To my beautiful wife,
Cherry,
whose constant encouragement,
helpful editing,
and consistent life
of Christian excellence
made this book possible.

Appendix E

Recent Books On Excellence

Bradford, David. *Managing for Excellence: The Guide to Developing High Performance in Contemporary Organizations*. New York: Wiley, 1984.

Egan, Gerard. *Change-Agent Skills: Assessing and Designing Excellence*. San Diego, University Associates, 1988.

Hanan, Mack. *Outperformers: Super-Achievers Breakthrough Strategies, High-Profit Results*. New York: AMACOM, 1989.

Inrig, Gary. *A Call to Excellence*. Wheaton, IL: Victor Books, 1985.

Johnston, Jon. *Stuck in a Sticky World: Learning to See God's Best in Life's Worst*. Joplin, MO: College Press, 1996.

Kushel, George. *Reaching the Peak Performance Zone: How to Motivate Yourself and Others to Excel*. New York: AMACOM, 1994.

Maehr, Martin L. *The Motivation Factor: A Theory of Personal Investment*. Lexington: Lexington Books, 1986.

Peters, Thomas. *Excellence in the Organization*. Chicago: Nightingale Conant, 1986. (sound recording)

Peters, Thomas. *Liberation Management: Necessary Disorganization for the Nanosecond Nineties*. New York: Knopf, 1987.

Peters, Thomas. *Thriving on Chaos: Handbook for a Management Revolution*. New York: Knopf, 1987.

Peters, Thomas. *The Tom Peters Seminar: Crazy Times Call for Crazy Organizations.* New York: Vintage Books, 1994.

Plimpton, George. *The X Factor: A Quest for Excellence.* New York: W. W. Norton, 1995.

Stinson, Gene. "A Call to Excellence." *Christian Standard.* June 23, 1996, pp. 8-10.

United States Department of Education. *Study of Excellence in High School Education: Longitudinal Study.* Washington, DC, Office of Educational Research and Improvement, 1982.

Waterman, Robert H. *Adhocracy: The Power to Change.* New York: W. W. Norton, 1992.

Waterman, Robert H. *The Renewal Factor: How the Best Get and Keep the Competitive Edge.* New York: Bantam Books, 1987.

CHRISTIAN EXCELLENCE

my gift to a
dear friend
and christian
brother.

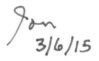
3/6/15

Proverbs 3:5-6

Other books by this author:

Stuck In A Sticky World: Learning To See God's Best In Life's Worst
Will Evangelicalism Survive Its Own Popularity?
Walls Or Bridges: How To Build Relationships That Glorify God
Courage: You Can Stand Strong In The Face Of Fear

CHRISTIAN EXCELLENCE

ALTERNATIVE TO SUCCESS

Second Edition

Jon Johnston

JKO Publishing, Inc.•200 Seaboard Lane•Franklin, TN 37067

Paperback edition
ISBN 0-9645014-4-9

Second edition, October 1996
Second printing, January 2004

Printed in the United States of America

General Editor: Kenneth W. Oosting, Ph.D.
Copy Editor: Amy Phillips, B.A.
Quality Control Coordinator: Kathy Zeigler, B.S.M.

Unless otherwise indicated, all Scripture references are from the Holy Bible:
New International Version, copyright © 1973, 1978 by the International Bible
Society.

The author wishes to express his appreciation for permission to reprint
"Success" by David Neff, by permission of *His*, student magazine of
InterVarsity Christian Fellowship, © 1984; the Temperament Test, taken from
After Every Wedding Comes A Marriage Workbook, copyright 1981, Harvest
House Publishers, 1075 Arrowsmith, Eugene, Oregon 97402; the Trenton
Spiritual Gifts Analysis, copyright Fuller Evangelistic Association, Box 989,
Pasadena, California 91102, no further reprint authorization is granted; and "I
Wonder" by Ruth Harms Calkin, from *Tell Me Again, Lord, I Forget*, published
by Tyndale House Publishing, Inc., © 1974 by Ruth Harms Calkin, used by
permission.

Order from:
JKO Publishing, Inc.
200 Seaboard Lane
Franklin, TN 37067
615/771-7705
Fax: 615/771-7810

Success is the key they hand you when they like you.
It doesn't matter why.
They just give you the key that unlocks an upscale condo,
triggers the powerful purr of your new Mercedes,
and accesses the executive washroom.
It's what they give to you.

Excellence is another brand of brazil nut.
It's what's within you.
It's what you do
that stretches mind and muscle.

They'll hand you success when your ratings are up,
your sales soar, or when the eager masses
plunk down their grubby bucks to buy your stuff.
And they'll snatch success away at daybreak.

Success loves its one-night stands at the Ritz.
But never expect it to say, I do.
Success is a day-tripper and a tease.
Success'll forget you.

Excellence endures when the crowd moves on.

David Neff

CONTENTS

Appendices

Foreword

Two dangers threaten the survival of Christendom. One is mediocrity; the other is success. We have been tempted by both of them. Jon Johnston, in this book, provides an alternative to either of them. That alternative is excellence.

Mediocrity has come to characterize the behavior of most people in most of our institutions. People grow up in homes with mediocre parents, receive a mediocre education, become mediocre in their productivity in industries that reek of mediocrity. They live out their Christian commitment in a mediocre fashion within the context of churches that have mediocre programs. It is not surprising that Jon Johnston, speaking as one committed to the Holiness tradition of Christianity, should find mediocrity to be intolerable. He refuses to allow the admonition of Christ to be "perfect" to be viewed as an unattainable goal that no one is expected to achieve, although nice to have for motivational purposes. Johnston makes it clear that excellence is a requirement of the Christian. To him, holiness is excellence. Love is excellence and being Christian is excellence.

In a Christian world, in which there has been an oversell of "cheap grace," Johnston reminds us that followers of Christ must "work out their own salvation" by developing the lifestyle that results in the maximum employment of one's gifts and service for others. He makes us see that godliness is a lifestyle in which a person is called to become all he or she can be in Christ.

Although Johnston is familiar with the literature on success, his viewpoint contrasts sharply. So far as Johnston is concerned, success, as this world understands it, is not the goal of the Christian. Wealth, power, and prestige, the common marks and symbols of worldly success, are not things that Christians are to aspire to possess. Instead, says Johnston, we are called to a simple lifestyle in which wealth is utilized to bless the less fortunate. Power is abandoned in adopting a lifestyle of servanthood, and prestige is discarded in favor of Christian humility. While rejecting the values of this world, Johnston makes it clear that we are still called to excellence. We are called to be efficient, committed, creative, and productive. However, all of these dimensions of personality are viewed in a different way as Johnston reinterprets them from a biblical perspective.

Evangelicalism continues to grow, especially in certain international areas (e.g., South Korea). Its numerical expansion and its heightened prestige have been conducive to the development of a "success theology." Those who propagate this new belief system argue that those who follow the teachings of Scripture and imitate Jesus will become a success in any ventures they enter. To become followers of Jesus means for the propagators of the success theology that Christians will be champions in athletics, victors in races for political office, winners of beauty contests, and leaders in business. They argue that the Christian lifestyle is a guaranteed route to the financial rewards that belong to the elite. Trusting in God will make all kinds of good things happen, from helping us to find parking places on crowded city streets to winning Olympic medals. Many contemporary revival meetings have the characteristics of Amway conventions. This is not surprising, since the principles of Scripture have been transformed into the criteria of success prescribed for Amway salespersons. All in all, Christianity has become a theodicy of good fortune for all too many in this second half of the twentieth century.

Over and against the success theology stands the work of Johnston. He helps us to remember that the followers of Jesus did not end up with expensive houses, money in the bank, and social prestige. He reminds us that the apostles, who, more than any since their day, have lived out the principles of God's Word in their imitation of their Master, ended up despised, rejected, impoverished, beaten, and eventually crucified. He reminds us that the excellence that is required of Christians in their everyday walk has no nexus with the success symbols which have increasingly become the symbols of "good" Christians.

Servanthood, powerlessness, and sacrifice are not prominent concepts in the mind-set of contemporary evangelicals. They know the words, but they do not know how to set them to music and hence they do not know how to play them out in the world. Johnston makes these traits core to the Christian lifestyle. He provides concrete direction for all who have chosen to follow Christ, our excellent example. The book is a call to servantlike, simple, sincere, inclusive, uncompromising, stewardly, and assertive excellence. It is a call to act with power and conviction. It is a challenge to change the world for Christ via the embracing of a value system of behavioral principles that many might consider countercultural.

Holiness is excellence, so there is no excuse for mediocrity. Success is worldly, so there is no excuse for Christians pursuing it. These are things that we must learn. These are things that Johnston teaches us effectively. In the words of the apostle Paul, we must, "press on toward the goal to win the prize for which God has called [us] heavenward in Christ Jesus" (Phil. 3:14). To all who would pursue this, the rest of the book will prove worthy.

Anthony Campolo, Jr.

Preface

L ike so many people, I once associated excellence with flawlessness. The excellent person never makes mistakes, is always consistent and confident, and is continuously applauded by scores of imperfect, jealous admirers.

My misconception produced guilt and disappointment as my shortcomings stubbornly lingered like barnacles on a pier. The gnawing thought persisted: I was destined to a life of ineptitude. As a result, I was bound to fail myself, others, and God. Before I could become fulfilled, something had to occur. Either I must drastically improve my level of performance, or I must take another look at the meaning of excellence.

In preparing the first edition, I began reading every book I could find on the subject of excellence. Many were helpful and informative, especially the Peters and Waterman classic, *In Search of Excellence*. These authors made the timeless virtue seem incredibly desirable and even attainable!

A truly abundant, significant, meaningful earthly life is possible. How could I, as a follower of the most excellent Person this world has ever known, ever doubt this fact?

But, like these authors—and most everyone I've ever met—my picture of excellence was cloudy and distorted. I failed to see the crucial distinction between excellence and success. The two seemed interchangeable.

Another book, Anthony Campolo's *Success Fantasy*, came to my attention. It provided the "corrective lens" for my distortion. I clearly understood that success motivation is an ego-driven compulsion to attain worldly goals—like feeling good, looking good and doing good.

The author vividly explained that God's children must focus on a much higher aspiration. One that can be condensed into one solid standard: excellence.

However, a penetrating thought came to mind: Perhaps others have likewise sought and found sustenance by exploring this concept. Perhaps they have perceptions they would be willing to share. The thought prompted action.

I contacted *Eternity*, which graciously loaned me its mailing list of the most noteworthy scholars and leaders of the evangelical world. To these gifted and dedicated Christians I sent a survey that contained three questions: What is Christian excellence? Why do you feel that it is so necessary today? What are the greatest barriers to attaining Christian excellence?

The response was overwhelming! College presidents, magazine editors, writers, and speakers of renown generously sent a great volume of valuable, God-inspired insights. It took weeks for me to carefully digest this information.

But, this survey was conducted a decade ago. After being requested to prepare a second edition of this book, I decided to consult influential scholars, leaders and practitioners once again. Some participated in the earlier study.

The questions posed were these:

1. Why does "excellence" persist as a theme in Christian books, conferences, etc.?
2. What special forms, or expressions, of Christian excellence are called for in the 90s—given the conditions of the world and the church?
3. What person, living today, would you select as "most reflecting the biblical meaning/practice of excellence"? Please share the basis for your choice. (See Appendix C.)

Once again, the information gleaned was insightful and inspirational. As in the book's first edition, I eagerly share what I have learned.

This book issues forth a warm invitation to journey on this less-traveled road. The road that leads to the "crown of glory that will never fade away" (1 Peter 5:4). My fervent prayer is that its pages will offer encouragement and guidance as we reach for, and grasp, our full spiritual potential. The One whose name is called "excellent" would have it so and promises to lovingly lead us in a "more excellent way" (1 Cor. 12:31, KJV).

Jon Johnston, Ph.D.
Pepperdine University
Malibu, California

Part 1

Excellence

Need of the World

Excellent things are as difficult as they are rare. — Baruch Spinoza

An excellent plumber is infinitely more admirable than an incompetent philosopher. — John W. Gardner, *Excellence: Can We Be Equal and Excellent Too?*

By expressing appreciation, we make excellence in others our property. — Voltaire

The older I get, the better I was! — bumpersticker

1

Enough Is Enough!

Any fiftieth wedding anniversary is a special occasion, especially when it involves your parents. And when your caring, perfectionist wife labors as hard as mine did to make the event successful, you hope that every detail will be right.

Nature did its best. It was a perfect day in Pasadena. All were in the best of spirits, especially my parents. The day was "one big smile" — almost. The florist forgot to deliver the flowers!

This was the one item that Cherry had arranged for months in advance. Everything had been neatly written out. She had made the customary triple-check and a telephone reminder just hours before the reception.

I can shut my eyes and again visualize all those bare tables, looking as blank as a plate of lard. The frustrated look in the eyes of my beautiful hostess, who struggled to maintain her characteristic poise and charm. The desperate attempt to pick flowers growing in the churchyard.

And one sight I shall never erase from my mind. The reception was over. The pictures had been taken. The awkward attempts to lessen the discomfort by making "flower jokes" had been made. In fact, everyone except the family had departed. Only we were standing there, dismantling the tables. In drove the delivery truck. Out stepped a red-faced man dressed in his golf outfit. His arms were filled with impeccable arrangements. This "picture of efficiency" quickly walked up to us and said, "So sorry. I promised my wife that I'd deliver these flowers on the way to play golf. I guess I just forgot."

What could we say? The very sight of this penitent in golf clothes, with some broken tees still poked in the side of his hat, could evoke only laughter. We forgave him and assured him that the occasion went well anyhow. We just thought we needed posies, when they were no doubt a foolish extra. He smiled and returned to his irate wife with his flowers and our request for a refund.

They're Out to Get Me

Such ineptness is repeated in my life on an almost daily basis. It began on the first day of my life, when they delivered my mother the wrong baby. She had to exchange that petite, beautiful female infant for me (no doubt reluctantly). It has been downhill ever since!

People constantly misspell my name. What's so confusing about the name *Jon Johnston*? Once I received an award. The first words were "Presented to John Jonston." Perhaps I expected too much. These people had known me for only five years. The alumni paper of my alma mater is addressed to Jonetta Johnson. If I were the sensitive type I'd be a candidate for psychotherapy.

And that's not all. Someone almost killed my beloved cat, Rerun. Before an extended trip, I painstakingly researched all sorts of animal-care facilities in our area. My investigation resulted in the selection of a prestigious animal clinic in the Malibu Hills area. Upon my return, I confidently drove to the facility and was greeted by what was left of my animal. Someone had forgotten to provide the advertised care by neglecting such "nonessential" items as food, water, bathing, and exercise. Just another example of nonexcellence!

Mastering the Art of Self-Destruction

To be fair, I must cease pointing my accusing finger at the rest of the world. My own life furnishes some remarkable examples of ineptitude: neglecting to preview a film for my church, a film that turned out to be risqué; wearing a wrong-color, wrong-style suit to a formal dinner at the Beverly Wilshire Hotel, and enduring those penetrating stares; tripping on the stage before thousands in the arena, and tens of thousands on television, just after receiving my Ph.D. diploma.

Many days I'm convinced that Murphy is my relative, maybe even my twin. Perhaps they also forgot to deliver him to my mother. You're familiar with his famous, constantly growing number of laws. Here are a few that I, especially, identify with:

> The other line always moves faster.
> The chance of the bread falling with the peanut-butter-and-jelly side down is directly proportionate to the cost of the carpet.
> Any tool dropped while repairing a car will roll underneath to the exact center.
> The repairman will never have seen a model quite like yours before.
> You remember you forgot to take out the trash when the garbage truck is two doors away.
> No matter how long or hard you shop for an item, after you've bought it, you'll find it somewhere else for a cheaper price.
> Friends come and go, but enemies accumulate.
> The light at the end of the tunnel is the headlamp of an oncoming train.[1]

Can you lay claim to being Murphy's kin? Or have you thought of instances of extreme ineptitude? If so, you will agree

---

[1]"Murphy's Law" (Millbrae, CA: Celestial Arts, 1979), quoted in Charles R. Swindoll, *Strengthening Your Grip: Essentials in an Aimless World* (Waco: Word, 1982), p. 211.

that excellence is needed in our day. Here we are speaking of secular excellence, excellence as a self-imposed standard of conduct. This means replacing bumbling with efficiency, carelessness with skill, embarrassment with pride.

In this day of technological sophistication, should not excellence characterize our society? The truth is, some people do excel, and in so doing become an inspiration for all of us.

The Few Whose Torches Are Lit

Martin Luther King, Jr., was right: We *can* overcome, despite adversity, the trend toward mediocrity, and the temptation to rationalize our weaknesses. You simply cannot keep a good person down.

> Cripple him, and you have a Sir Walter Scott.
> Lock him in a prison cell, and you have a John Bunyan.
> Bury him in the snows of Valley Forge, and you have a George Washington.
> Raise him in abject poverty, and you have an Abraham Lincoln.
> Strike him down with infantile paralysis, and he becomes a Franklin D. Roosevelt.
> Burn him so severely that the doctors say he'll never walk again, and you have a Glenn Cunningham who set the world's one-mile record in 1934.
> Deafen him and you have a Ludwig van Beethoven.
> Have him or her born black in a society filled with racial discrimination, and you have a Booker T. Washington, a Marian Anderson, a George Washington Carver, or a Martin Luther King, Jr.
> Call him a slow learner, "retarded," and write him off as uneducable, and you have an Albert Einstein.[2]

We see examples of excellence all around us. These persons, measuring themselves by themselves, set high standards. They know the fulfillment that accompanies attainment whether it means playing the piano like Peter Nero or being a dependable

---

[2]Quoted in Ted W. Engstrom, *The Pursuit of Excellence* (Grand Rapids: Zondervan, 1982), p. 1.

custodian like Rosie Sanchez who cleans my office. These people, as Alfred North Whitehead would term it, "cultivate the habitual vision of greatness" every day.

Indefinable But Within Reach

Excellence is difficult to define. But we all certainly recognize it when we observe it in others. And we are refreshed and reassured when we witness it. What is excellence? It's a certain style of life, a manner of living, a bigness of spirit, a point of view, a frame of reference, a set of priorities, a hierarchy of values, an admirable self-imposed standard.[3]

As John W. Gardner says, we cannot "expect every man to be excellent.... But many more can achieve it than now do. Many, many more can try to achieve it than now do. And the society is bettered not only by those who achieve it but by those who are trying."[4]

Some people wince at the very mention of excellence. Pursuing excellence is like beginning a journey. To embark on this journey necessitates facing unresolved pain and stubborn weaknesses.

Others begin the journey with the best of intentions, only to succumb later to the fatal disease of "unrealistic expectations." In some cases, these expectations were purposely placed beyond reach in order to cushion the effect of inevitable failure. Still others feign excellence, going through the motions to impress. But, their day of revelation is inevitable. If only some of these disheartened ones could come to believe three truths.

First, every person, no matter how lowly, has the potential to attain excellence. In *Letters to His Son*, Lord Chesterfield writes, "There is scarcely anybody who is absolutely good for nothing, and hardly anybody good at everything."[5]

---

[3]C. William Fisher, *Our Goal Is Excellence* (Kansas City, MO: Beacon Hill, n.d.), p. 13.

[4]John W. Gardner, *Excellence: Can We Be Equal and Excellent Too?* (New York: Harper and Row, 1961), p. 133.

[5]Quoted in Engstrom, *The Pursuit of Excellence*, p. 84.

Second, involvement in the process of attaining excellence is intensely satisfying to the human spirit. Growth is its own reward; to cease growing is to start dying. On the inside cover of his Bible Oliver Cromwell had penned, *"Qui cessat esse melior cessat esse bonus."* (He who ceases to better ceases to be good.)[6]

Third, excellence guarantees results! Attaining excellence is no empty ritual. Eventually it pays off. It improves individuals, but the ripple effect is also felt by all of society. Airplanes become safe. Clothes sent to the cleaners are returned cleaned. Restaurant food no longer tastes bland.

We're not speaking of crisis excellence which Chrysler was made to resort to when the company was teetering on the brink of bankruptcy. Nor are we referring to the obsessive, workaholic-type excellence that reflects a sickness of mind and emotions.

Instead, we're speaking of a voluntary, flowing, constantly improving excellence that corresponds with the rhythm of our nature. This is an excellence that strives for more than "getting by," that is concerned with "being" as well as "doing." It is an excellence that is within the reach of everyone from a large corporation like General Motors ("Ours is the way of excellence") to the Honda worker in Tokyo, who, on his lunch break, walks down the street straightening the windshield wipers on every parked Honda he encounters.[7]

If excellence is this great, why don't we hear more about it? Because we hear so much about success.

---

[6]Quoted in William Barclay, *The Daily Study Bible: The Letter to the Hebrews* (Philadelphia: Westminster, 1955), p. 52.

[7]Thomas J. Peters and Robert H. Waterman, Jr., *In Search of Excellence: Lessons from America's Best-Run Companies* (New York: Harper and Row, 1982), p. 37. On this same page, Peters and Waterman ask, "What exactly, is the nature of Japan's magic?" Then they quote Fortune: "The Japanese deserve credit for far more than the circumstantial triumph of being able to supply efficient cars to a country [the United States] caught short of them. They excel in the quality of fits and finishes, moldings that match, doors that don't sag, materials that look good and wear well, flawless paint jobs. Most important of all, Japanese cars have earned a reputation for reliability, borne out by the generally lower rate of warranty claims they experience. Technically, most Japanese cars are fairly ordinary."

Aren't excellence and success the same? Many think so, but they are not. In fact, they are opposites in many respects. Not only that, but they are often enemies also.

The highest offices of the state and church resemble a pyramid whose top is accessible to only two sorts of animals — eagles and reptiles. — John Wesley

Since failure is our unforgivable sin, we are willing to ignore all forms of deviance in people if they just achieve the success symbols which we worship. — Anthony Campolo, *The Success Fantasy*

The pressure to succeed is greater that it has ever been.... People feel that they must pursue that goal even if it means crawling over the bodies of coworkers or sacrificing what they really want. — Paul Rosch, President, American Institute of Stress

It is wonderful to be famous, as long as you remain unknown. — Dega

2

Competing Ideals

Excellence and Success

John Mason Brown has written, "Existence is a strange bargain. Life owes us little; we owe it everything. The only true happiness comes from squandering ourselves for a purpose."[8]

Man's energies and creativity are mainly devoted to achieving two key purposes: excellence and success. There is usually some overlap. People who focus on one frequently attain a

---

[8]Quoted in John W. Gardner, *Excellence: Can We Be Equal and Excellent Too?* (New York: Harper and Row, 1961), p. 149.

measure of the other. Again, we are speaking of excellence from a secular standpoint.[9] At this point it might be helpful to examine both success and excellence. Such a comparison will provide a greater understanding of each.

Success: A Pot of Gold

For purposes of discussion, let us establish the term success as attaining cultural goals that are sure to elevate one's perceived importance within that culture. In practical terms, it means an elevation in power (having commands obeyed and wishes granted); in privilege (being given special rights or favors); or in wealth (accumulating financial reserves and the accompanying security).[10]

To a degree, every person is successful. But the term is most often reserved for those who "have it made," or are "making it big." Such persons wear clothing with the right labels, eat at the best restaurants, and sit in the most expensive seats at the most exclusive social events. One person summarized the principle well: "Success is what your meat cutter would have if he were a surgeon."

Part of my wife's compensation as a travel consultant is in the form of passes to stay at resort hotels. One Christmas we stayed at one of Waikiki's newest and most prestigious hotels. We experienced a few days of luxury befitting a V.I.P.

It began when our taxi pulled up to unload. A virtual army of attendants simultaneously opened all the car doors and the trunk. Bags disappeared in a flash. I still can't figure out how everyone knew our names without our telling them. No waiting at a registration desk for us! Instead, we were immediately escorted to the $220-per-night room. At our bedroom desk we quickly registered as we consumed Swiss chocolates that had been delivered to our palatial quarters.

---

[9]It stands to reason that if a person excels, he is frequently successful. Also, the encouragement generated from being successful often motivates one increasingly to excel.

[10]Wealth, in this context, is both earned income and unearned gifts. In terms of status, the latter is more significant than the former. "New money" is often perceived as unworthy of attention; instead, the family name gains one entrance in the higher strata of society.

Tough life indeed! But one to which I, increasingly, found myself wanting to become accustomed. It was hard to pry away from such luxuries and resume living at home again, where there were no more chocolates or maids. The ultimate sacrifice was no more evening turndown of the bed—along with the accompanying pillow-gifts of a seashell and an orchid. Have I evoked your deepest sympathy?

I was being treated like a successful person, and I loved it—though to use biblical language, it "came to pass" and was but "for a season."

Success is society telling you that you've arrived, then treating you as if people believe it. No wonder people are driving themselves so hard to achieve it! It beats scrubbing bathrooms, wearing rags, and waiting in welfare lines. A person has to be crazy to opt for noncomfort, unspecial treatment, an unspectacular existence.

Anthony Campolo, Jr., describes the extent to which success has captivated Americans:

> Success is a shining city, a pot of gold at the end of the rainbow. We dream of it as children, we strive for it through our adult lives, and we suffer melancholy in old age if we have not reached it.
>
> Success is the place of happiness. And the anxieties we suffer at the thought of not arriving there give us ulcers, heart attacks, and nervous disorders. If our reach exceeds our grasp, and we fail to achieve what we want, life seems meaningless and we feel emotionally dead.[11]

In an article in *People*, Brad Darrach poses the rhetorical question: "Why does the world's biggest crowd of celebrities pay millions for dime-size lots in a perilous, polluted 'paradise'?"[12] The answer is obvious: to appear successful. I know because I'm a professor at a university in Malibu—within a stone's throw from "the Colony," as it is called. I see the super-rich as they leisurely stroll through the old-world shops—"dripping with gold jewelry" and purchasing whatever they desire. Cost is no consideration.

---

[11]Anthony Campolo, Jr., *The Success Fantasy* (Wheaton: Victor, 1980), p. 9.
[12]Brad Darrach, "Malibu," *People*, 1 August 1983, p. 51.

People affected by the "success fantasy" either live in places like Malibu, Beverly Hills, or Manhattan, or else constantly dream about it. They wish, hope, envy, or connive. Perhaps the last are the ones who should be most pitied. Their affections are set on an elusive dream.

How then does the motivation to succeed contrast with that to excel? What is the essential difference?

Excellence: The Rainbow

It is a well-known and accepted fact that our brain never really conceptualizes something until it contrasts that something with something else. For example, someone tells you that you're "pretty." Compared with what? Miss America? An orangutan? A person assures you that you're "smart." Compared with Albert Einstein, or a child in kindergarten? The last time I went to the dentist, I confidently declared that I had kept my mouth very clean. My dentist smiled and retorted, "Jon, a human's mouth is a virtual cesspool of germs—second only to that of a camel in terms of filth." I thereafter revised my claim to say I maintain a clean mouth—compared with a camel's.

Similarly, our comprehension of excellence is enhanced by contrasting it with something we constantly hear about: success.

Please keep in mind that there is some overlap between the two. Also, I am not implying that one is invariably good and the other is always undesirable. Much depends on our motive. In addition, realize that there is little consensus among those who have attempted to define these concepts. Therefore, I am taking the liberty to furnish my own definitions. The following are the differences that I perceive. Finally, remind yourself that we are speaking of these ideals from a secular point of view, although there are obvious spiritual overtones.

Success is based upon attaining a hoped-for future goal.

Excellence provides a striven-for present standard.

Success bases our worth on a comparison with others.

Excellence gauges our value by measuring us against our own potential.

Success grants its rewards to the few, but
multitudes.

Excellence is available to all living bei'
the special few.

Success focuses its attention on the external — be
tastemaker for the insatiable appetites of the conspi
consumer.

Excellence beams its spotlight on the internal spirit —
becoming the quiet, but pervasive, conscience of the conscientious who yearn for integrity.

Success engenders fantasy and a compulsive groping for the
pot of gold at the end of the rainbow.

Excellence brings us to reality, and a deep gratitude for the
affirming promise of the rainbow.

Success encourages expedience and compromise, which
prompts us to treat people as a means to our end.

Excellence cultivates principles and consistency, which
ensure that we will treat all persons as intrinsically
valuable ends — the apex of our heavenly Father's creation.

It is evident that success pales in the brilliance of excellence.
The latter, in comparison with the former, is an essential ingredi-
ent in the character of any nation. To attain it is to survive and
continually to improve. To lack it is, at best, merely to exist and
inevitably to shrink to a deplorable nothingness.

Therefore, in our world, excellence must not be perceived as
optional. It is a necessity. The same cannot be said for success.
Even perishing societies have successful people. But, lacking
excellence, whose fate is sealed.

Excellence is always expensive — whether in a house, car,
rocket, or mousetrap. It is never on sale. Those who attain excellence must pay the full cost — in time, in effort, in resources. That

means enduring a rejection that inevitably accompanies
ıg out of rank in the world's parade in order to march with
w to the beat of another drummer. But excellence is well worth
.he sacrifice. It is far more valuable than any form of fleeting success.

The poet James Russell Lowell provides words that beauti-
fully summarize this principle:

> Life is a leaf of paper white
> Whereon each one of us may write
> His word or two,
> And then comes night.
>
> Greatly begin, though thou have time
> But for a line,
> Be that sublime,
> *Not failure, but low aim, is crime.* [13]

---

[13]Quoted in Ted W. Engstrom, *The Pursuit of Excellence* (Grand Rapids: Zondervan, 1982), p. 92.

Excellent things are rare. —Plato, *The Republic*

... it seems to me, each individual amongst us could in his own person, with the utmost grace and versatility prove himself self-sufficient in the most varied forms of activity. —Pericles, funeral oration

He who knows Palestine and Greece knows the germ of four-fifths or more of western civilization, and has seen its animating and sustaining forces in their simplest and purest forms. —R. W. Livingstone, *Greek Ideals and Modern Life*

Athens, the source whence civilization, knowledge, religion, agriculture, justice, and law have sprung and spread into all lands. —Cicero

3

The Greeks Had a Word for It

He grimaces with pain. Veins protrude in his neck. Every leg muscle strains to the limit. His lungs feel like they're in flames. The sprinter, who has trained arduously for this moment of truth, suddenly spurts ahead of the other runners and crosses the finish line with a final burst of energy. He has won the race, but receives no gold medal, only a simple garland cut with a golden sickle. He climbs no victor's platform to accept the crowd's acclaim. Instead, he bows at a nearby shrine, dedicated to his warrior god, Zeus, to offer a quiet prayer of gratitude.

The year is 776 B.C. The place is the sacred plain of Olympia.

Almost three millennia later, I stood with my university students beside the ruins of the ancient track. Our guide, Olympia's mayor, provided a vivid mental journey into the past:

The Games were primarily worship rituals to honor the gods of Greek mythology. That is why the premises were crowded with altars, statues, and sacred mounds.[14]

No women were allowed among the twenty thousand spectators. Any discovered were put to death.[15]

Runners wore no clothes, and even greased down their bodies to reduce wind resistance.

Just prior to the Games, nobles from Elis journeyed to all Greek cities to proclaim *ekecheiria*, a cessation of all hostilities for a period of three months.

As he dramatized, I couldn't help contrasting the scene he described with the Olympics of our day. Certainly the ancient Greeks weren't concerned with boycotts, drug tests, television by satellite, bribery, hostage seizing, or asylum seeking.

Admittedly, participants desired to win, but not in order to declare, "Hey, world, look what I did!" They did not hope to receive a call from the country's president, nor to land a professional contract with a seven-figure-salary.[16]

---

[14]This was originally a religious shrine, dedicated to exalting the gods and honoring the deceased. At the Great Altar of Zeus the accumulated ashes of the sacrificed animals gradually formed a seven-meter-high mound. The sacred flame burned within the Enclosure of Zeus, a circle of upright slabs, where an oracle spoke through the movements of the sacrificial bull's skin. *Touring Greece* (Athens: Editions K. Gouvoussis, n.d.), pp. 63-67. Apart from the Great Altar of Zeus, where the richest sacrifices were offered, there were many altars. Pausanias mentions sixty-nine. Manolis Andronicos, *Olympia* (Athens: Ekdotike Athenon S.A., n.d.), p. 6.

[15]There was one exception to this rule. One beauty queen, representative of the gods, was allowed to witness the events. She was given all the privileges of a high-school homecoming queen.

[16]The Games took place under the gaze and protection of the warrior god Zeus, according to Greek legend. He was believed to be the one who always stood by the Hellenes, whether in the struggles of war or in the peaceful athletic contests. In return, the Greeks, being a deeply religious people, offered him the arms which had brought them victory and the spoils of war which the god had helped them appropriate. All victors set up their own statues in the shrine of Zeus, not out of arrogance, but with the piety of those who can accept a god's gift in perfect humility. As the years went by, the votive offerings in the sacred grove

What motivated the ancient Olympic athletes? What drove them toward sacrificial preparation during the years of their youth? To willingly accept long hours of training in the scorching Mediterranean sun?

The All-Consuming Ambition

One obsession burned within the breast of all Olympic competitors—namely, the yearning for meaningful excellence. Excellence was more precious, it was thought, than costly gems, wealth, or unbounded power.

What held true for these athletes was also a reality for other walks of life: philosophers like Aristotle, savage fighters like Diomede, poverty-stricken peasants like Hesiod, even Athenian youth who flocked to Sophists in order to be guided toward the ideal.

It was the intentional aim of the ancient Greek society to achieve excellence, in spite of the fact that the culture was steeped in superstition. Is it any wonder that excellence has been termed the "instinct of the Greek race" or that it is discussed in the earliest literature of that ancient civilization? Plato gave much thought to it, as did Homer and most other authors. The ideal of achieving excellence was the very cornerstone of ancient Hellenic society.

Today we're quite impressed by the concept of excellence, which most dictionaries define as superiority. We smile when our boss tells us that we have performed in an excellent manner or when the coach says we have excelled. And who hasn't seen movies about European kings who were addressed by the pompous title *Your Excellency*?

We might have a pretty good idea of what we mean by excellence. But what exactly did the Greeks mean when they used the word? Did they mean what we mean or something more?

---

grew so numerous that they could be numbered in the thousands. They included precious and famed trinkets of war and games that resulted in Olympia becoming the most complete museum of Greek history. Andronicos, *Olympia,* p. 16.

Arete: The Ultimate's Ultimate

Words can be mighty. "Freedom" has been the rally cry for many wars, as have "Fatherland" and "destiny." But few words in the annals of history have carried the rich meaning of *arete*, the Greek term for excellence. In some contexts it suggests "virtue"; in others "superiority"; in still others "preeminence" and even "perfection."[17]

Think of the ultimate of which mankind is capable. Then, add still more because of the limitation of your mind. Now you have but a shadowy idea of the concept's meaning.

R. W. Livingstone's understanding of *arete* is illuminating:

> It is the belief that man is more important than his environment or his possessions, and that his fundamental business is not to understand nature, though this is one of his problems, nor to earn a livelihood, though that is one of his duties, but so to lead his life as to [attain] ... all of what is characteristic of, peculiar to, and highest in human nature; or, as the Greeks put it, to achieve the *arete* of man.[18]

An inspiring concept to be sure, and one that the ancient Greeks were driven to attain. But why? What is the magnetic appeal of excellence? Just what was it about this ideal that was considered so inviting and rejuvenating?

To put it simply, the contemplation of *arete* had a way of generating awesome power for the ancient Greeks. It had power to draw men away from lesser aims to follow after it. The best, when conceptualized, was desired and sought. To realize that man had a perfection generated creative and energetic activity. As one author put it: "The mere idea of human perfection constituted a self-evident claim on the human spirit."[19]

The concept had power to develop conceptions of good from lower to higher, in a vision that was progressively purified and enlarged as human experience grew. There was nothing fixed

---

[17]R. W. Livingstone, *Greek Ideals and Modern Life* (London: Oxford University Press, n.d.), pp. 69-72.

[18]Ibid., p. 88.

[19]Ibid., p. 77.

nor static in *arete*! The ideal grew as the intellect grew and rose as high as the imagination could take it.

Arete also had power to broaden perspective so that narrowness and provincialism vanished. Unlike most societies, which are afflicted by the "prison of the tribal, and the intellectual tyranny of the contemporary,"[20] ancient Greeks saw life as life — with all of its diversities, dimensions, and complexities.

Finally, the concept had power to attract men to the inherent value of itself. It was addictive. When authentic excellence was seen in all of its radiant beauty, it became its own reward. Rather than being primarily valued for its products — be they wealth, architecture, or Olympic victory — excellence was prized for itself. Involvement in the process of attaining it became intensely gratifying. This feeling is evident in these lines:

> How good is man's life, the mere living!
> How fit to employ all the soul and the mind
> and the senses forever in joy![21]

Arete generated spectacular accomplishments among the ancient Greeks. In addition, their excellence produced an awesome effect.

The Lingering Legacy

The Greek civilization became, without a doubt, the most admired and imitated of all of human history.

Hear Johann Wolfgang von Goethe as he declares, "Of all peoples the Greeks have dreamt of life best."[22] Or Percy Bysshe Shelley as he says, "What we are and hope to be is derived from the influence and inspiration of these glorious generations."[23] Or Alexander von Humboldt as he states, "No other people has combined simplicity and naturalness with so high a culture. The

---

[20]This phrase is often used in anthropology to single out the two manifestations of the stereotype-prejudice-discrimination syndrome, which leads to ethnocentrism. These manifestations are relinquishing individuality to group goals, and basing all values, norms, and status on present-day tastes and fads.

[21]Livingstone, *Greek Ideals and Modern Life*, p. 79.

[22]Quoted, ibid., p. 43.

[23]Ibid.

state of Athens at its climax, that is of human nature at its climax."[24]

Because we are so product-oriented, our admiration is mainly directed toward the Greeks' physical creations: the philosophical and scientific writings; the intricately carved statues from which Michelangelo took his cues; the classic architecture, which is the model for the facades of our courthouses.

As impressive as Greek civilization is, the ancient Hellenic legacy provides mankind with an even greater gift, a profound perspective which fascinates the imagination and kindles the soul—the ideal of excellence. To fully grasp this view of life is to experience true renaissance, regardless of the spatial or temporal setting.

---

[24]Ibid.

When we realize this fact, crucial questions come to mind: How did the Greek ideal of excellence filter into God's Word? In what ways was its meaning altered?

Let's focus on answers to these important questions.

Part **2**

Excellence

Norm of God's Word

*Let us thank God that he makes us live among the present problems....
It is no longer permitted to anyone to be mediocre.* —Pope Pius XI

*A Christian should constantly seek ... highest standards and employ
the most demanding comparisons for [his self-] evaluations.* —
J. Richard Chase

*It is particularly significant that Christ's people, who have tasted
immortal knowledge, serve him with excellence.* —J. Kenneth Grider

*The early Christian church conquered because the Christians of those
days out-thought, out-lived, and out-died the pagans.* —T. R. Glover

4

Understanding With An Open Mind

It's amusing to watch foreigners try to communicate when they can't speak the language. The same few words are loudly repeated over and over in an unintelligible accent and with plenty of vigorous hand motions.

As a traveler to a distant land, it is awkward to be forced to use such tactics. But it would seem even more difficult if you were attempting to converse with foreigners in your homeland, especially when such aliens are considered intruders by your closest friends!

Jesus found himself in such a situation. He no doubt came into frequent contact with Greeks and Greek-speaking Jews. After all, his boyhood town of Nazareth was but two miles south of Sepphoris, the "all-Greek" capital of Herod Antipas.

Our Lord may have belonged to a family and community of Jews who tenaciously clung to their Jewishness. Nevertheless, such people must have been like an island in a sea of Greek customs and ideas. It is possible that our Lord spoke a broken Greek—similar to a foreign shopkeeper's broken English. Certainly he was fully aware of the impact of Greek thinking on Jewish life.[25]

That influence had deeply penetrated Israel. Three centuries had passed since the days when the greatest of all Greek commanders, Alexander, had invaded and conquered their land (332 B.C.). That same influence lasted about another six centuries, until the time of the Arab takeover (A.D. 636).[26]

After enduring Jewish rejection, it is little wonder that Jesus increasingly directed his ministry to the Greeks. He journeyed to their cities: Bethsaida, Caesarea Philippi, and the coastal town of Tyre, as well as the great cities (Decapolis) near the Sea of Galilee. This ministry intensified until the Jews reacted with anger, seeing him much as a Klansman might see a Mississippi white man who accepted a black man's invitation to dinner.

Following Christ's example, the early church continued to focus attention on Greeks. When it came time to pen his inspired letters to the churches, Paul wrote in Greek—because he was writing mostly to Greeks. Although Paul sought to reach both

---

[25]Although his archaeological focus has been near the Sea of Galilee, primarily at Tel Hum (Capernaum) and Banias (Caesarea Phillipi), John Wilson states that first-century Jewish graves throughout the entire region are inscribed in Greek. His point: The language people think in is, as an archaeological rule, the language they select for their tombstones. Wilson's observation about Palestine also holds true for the first-century Jews buried in foreign lands. "The dominant position of Greeks among the Jews of the Diaspora may be seen from a study of catacomb inscriptions from Rome, which shows that seventy-four percent were in Greek, twenty-four percent in Latin, and only two percent in Hebrew or Aramaic." Harry J. Leon, *The Jews of Rome* (Philadelphia: Jewish Publication Society, 1961), quoted in Donald J. Wiseman and Edwin Yamauchi, *Archaeology and the Bible: An Introductory Study* (Grand Rapids: Zondervan, 1979), p. 66. The influence of Greek thinking on Christ's world must have been great and related to all areas.

[26]Although the zionistic Maccabees successfully expunged the land of foreigners (160 B.C.), even they remained Greek in language and thought. The rule of Roman Caesars, Herods, and governors (47 B.C. onward) was likewise Hellenistic.

Jews and Greeks, he discovered among cosmopolitan Greeks a far greater potential for spreading the gospel than among the Hebrews.

But what about the Greek words that Paul and other biblical writers used? Words that we believe to be inspired and inspiring? Words that we live by? Are the meanings of such Greek words tainted by pagan Greek philosophy?

Biblical authors, guided by God's Spirit, added a new dimension to Greek concepts and words.[27] One such word is *arete*, Greek for "excellence." As we have noted, the ancient Greeks accorded the concept great significance, so that the effort to attain to excellence became the virtual bedrock of their civilization. The word referred to the ultimate of what is characteristic of or peculiar to the highest in human nature. The ancient Greeks believed that the greatest manifestation of excellence is possessing profound wisdom. For wisdom, the queen of the virtues, is the gateway to the good, the true, the beautiful.

This is impressive, perhaps even awesome, when you think of what the concept helped the Greeks accomplish. But the writers of God's Word used *arete* to describe other concepts and qualities. Excellence became intimately associated with the daily Christian walk. Christians were given a motivating, enriching, but attainable standard providing full access to the victorious life.

The Metamorphosis of a Concept

What, then, does excellence — as it is described in the Bible — mean for the Christian? Influential Christian scholars and leaders

---

[27]A prime illustration of this is the Greek word *logos*, which implied truth, logic, and symmetry. Ancient Greeks placed the word in the context of an abstract, philosophical idea upon which the world existed. New Testament writers expanded the term to mean the living, dynamic person of Jesus Christ, who embodies all the Greeks meant and much more (John 1:1-5). Another example is *pistis*, the Greek word for faith. Whether used narrowly as a philosophical term, or in the vernacular, it suggested a man-generated confidence based on trust in his own abilities. Biblical authors employed the term to mean a deep trust based on the abiding assurance that our Lord strengthens us from within (Heb. 11; 12:2; 1 Peter 1:5). He is the Vine. We are the branches that draw sustenance from the Vine (John 15:5). As a result, we can be sure that our fruit-bearing potential is as limitless as his inexhaustible power and infinite wisdom.

replied to this question in a recent survey that I administered. Their answers were enlightening.

> Following out to its end the intrinsic character of a quality, event, or mode of being, and seeing this pursuit in light of ... the resurrection — that all things cohere in Christ. — Martin Marty
>
> Doing all to the glory of God, which requires my best. — Hudson Armerding
>
> Discovering who we are as Christ's people, and committing ourselves to live out his radical servant lifestyle within the body of Christ. — Larry Richards
>
> There is no such thing as Christian excellence, just as there is no Christian hamburger; but a Christian will strive for excellence (i.e., integrity) with every task he attempts. It could mean making the very best hamburger you can with plenty of onion, tomato, and pickle. — Haddon Robinson
>
> Wholism, or seeing the whole of life as subject to the lordship of Jesus Christ, may be at the core of Christian excellence. And at the center of such wholism is wholesomeness. — David Moberg

All of these definitions focus on important elements of excellence for the Christian: glorifying God, being servants, seeing things in light of the resurrection, having integrity, and being wholistic and wholesome in attitude. Thus, "excellence" is an umbrella term. That is why *arete* can be translated to mean "virtue," a general term, in addition to "excellence."

But it must be understood that the most important dimension of excellence is *agape* love, the supreme virtue. Mark Moore put it well: "It is as we improve the expression of God-given love that we come to realize the standard of Christian excellence."

Paul declares, "And now these three [cardinal virtues] remain: faith, hope and love. But the greatest of these is (*agape*) love" (1 Cor. 13:13). Perhaps that is because, as J. Kenneth Grider states, "Of the three, only love will not cease in the next world." Or, as has also been suggested, maybe love is a summation of all the other virtues.

This same thirteenth chapter of First Corinthians is universally known as the "love chapter" of God's Word. Generations have received instruction and inspiration from its wise and uplifting thoughts. Without a doubt, it is a "Gibralter of our faith." It is important to note that Paul's profound teaching on the supremacy of love is introduced with words that clearly reveal an inseparable link between excellence and love: "And now I [Paul] will show you the most excellent way" (1 Cor. 12:31). What is it? The way of love.[28]

The Bible is emphatic. If we desire excellence—the kind of excellence that will bring the most glory to our heavenly Father—we must deepen in our understanding of, and commitment to, authentic *agape* love, a love that is unconditional, sacrificial, and available to all.

Available to all. Now there's an inspiring thought! What a contrast to the excellence of the ancient Greeks: excellence equated with great powers of reason. That excellence would be restricted to the few born with an extraordinary mind and given the opportunity to develop it.[29] By contrast, Christian excellence

---

[28]Equating excellence with *agape* love is this author's understanding of the connoted definition of *arete*. Theologians-exegetes Ralph Earle, W. T. Purkiser, and J. Kenneth Grider, when queried, concurred with this understanding. Although biblical excellence is not only *agape* love, it is the latter in its most refined sense. W. E. Vine provides a specific definition: "Arete properly denotes whatever procures pre-eminent estimation for a person or thing; hence, intrinsic eminence, moral goodness, virtue, (a) of God ... (b) of any particular moral excellence ... where virtue is enjoined as an essential quality in the exercise of faith." W. E. Vine, *An Expository Dictionary of New Testament Words* (Old Tappan, NJ: Revell, 1966), pp. 189-190.

[29]To illustrate, according to Aristotle, several conditions must be present before *arete* can exist. He states, "Evidently it [i.e., *arete*] needs external goods as well; for it is impossible or not easy to do what is noble unless furnished with external means. There are many things that can only be done through the instrumentality of friends or wealth or political power; and there are some things, such as good birth, good looks and good children, the lack of which take the lustre from happiness." Thus, to the Greek, *arete* required more than a usual endowment of intelligence. That intelligence had to be cultivated or developed with the support of such ideal conditions. If one is aware of this and other radical contrasts between ancient Greek and biblical concepts of excellence, it is understandable that some scholars would overreact by opposing all Greek ideas in God's Word. Such was the position of Rudolf Bultmann and other liberal German theologians who held that all that Jesus said is good, but all other biblical instruction is tainted by Greek influence (e.g., doctrine of the Trinity). According

is within everyone's reach: philosopher and artist, but also the illiterate and impoverished; gold medalists and people who never get to be first in anything. Even the most obscure and insignificant persons can possess an overflowing, unpretentious, and genuine love. In fact, Christ's Sermon on the Mount seems to say that such people are closer to such love than those of great power and wealth (Matt. 5:3-11).

Christian excellence is based upon *agape* love. But what else is said about excellence in God's Word?

The Source and Supplier of Excellence: God

Excellence describes the very nature of God. The psalmist declared, "How excellent is thy name [i.e., nature] in all the earth" (8:1, KJV).[30]

Furthermore, the excellence of our heavenly Father is closely intertwined with his glory. The Hebrew word for "glory" (*hod*), in reference to God, is translated *arete* by writers of the Septuagint (see Hab. 3:3; Zech. 6:13). The scholars believed that our Creator's glory is best described by the Greek word for excellence.

So we can conclude that God's glory is his excellence! And his excellence is his glory. Not incidentally, that is closely related to the Bible's straightforward statement that "God is love" (1 John 4:7), the divine embodiment of true excellence.

We find ourselves asking how we, who are plagued with so many inglorious frailties and limitations, can meaningfully relate to the glorious, excellent one.

---

to this view, the Greeks, who pervasively appeared on the scene after Christ's death, brought distortion and error. As a result, their additions ruined the original Semitic simplicity of Holy Writ. Therefore we cannot legitimately accept the Book of Acts and other Scripture that has been infiltrated by their heretical thoughts. On the surface, this position may appear plausible. However, on closer inspection, it is accurately seen as a baseless rationalization providing license to reject inspired sections of our Bible. As Wilson states, "Christianity was *always* a form of Hellenistic Judaism. There was no abrupt movement from Jewishness to Greekness." With this in mind, we are justified in accepting the totality of Scripture with clear conscience and sound reason.

[30]In Hebrew society, and throughout most cultures of the ancient world, a person's name was thought to connote his identity. Hence, upon his conversion, the name Saul was changed to "Paul." When we are told that God's name is Excellence, we realize that this means his entire nature is permeated with excellence.

"Where He Leads" is a favorite hymn of mine—especially the fourth stanza which asserts, "He will give me grace and glory."[31] It is wonderful to know that God is excellent and glorified, but to know that he will share excellence with us is no less than inspiring. How is this possible? Because he is the supreme wellspring of grace and glory, we know that these gifts are his to give. To discover that his glory and excellence are inseparable is to treasure the song's words and his generous gift even more.

Reflect on this a moment. Rather than hoarding his radiant excellence, our God lovingly offers to bestow it upon us, his rebellious and undeserving creation. It is with good reason that Peter triumphantly declares, "For His divine power has bestowed upon us every requisite for life and goodness, through knowing Him who called us to His own glory and excellence" (2 Peter 1:3, NBV). This is excellence that defies adequate description and stretches our imaginations.

In sharp contrast, the Greeks believed that excellence was based on the sheer efforts of man. Through his own efforts, man could fashion an elaborate ethical system that would enable him to develop his potential. As he plodded along on his path toward excellence he might eventually discover some mysterious, impersonal god-source. But he shouldn't count on it. For the ancient Greeks, the journey toward excellence began with the visible and moved toward the invisible; from humanity to deity.

This is not so with Christian excellence. God's Word assures us of more than a hope in finding our Maker at the end of the road—provided we have attained excellence. Instead, we can know that the Father of all excellence—whose nature and will are revealed to all who have receptive hearts—joins us at the beginning of our journey. With each step he provides strength for the next one.

Thoughts That Soothe and Comfort

As we open the doors of our hearts (see Rev. 3:20) to receive divine excellence, we find ourselves yearning to apply that gift to every area of our life.

---

[31]John S. Norris and E. W. Blandly, *Worship in Song* (Kansas City, MO: Lillenas, 1972), p. 397.

Such application begins with a radical purging of our minds. Unclean thoughts must go. Jesus once declared that evil thoughts proceed from the heart (Matt. 15:19). This implies that as our hearts are filled with his love, our thoughts will become pure.

God's Word proclaims that we are judged, in part, by the thoughts and attitudes of our hearts (Heb. 4:12). Why are thoughts so crucial? They are the prelude to attitudes, words, actions.

Paul instructed all believers with these words: "whatever is true, whatever is noble, whatever is right, whatever is pure, whatever is lovely, whatever is admirable — if anything is excellent or praiseworthy — think about such things" (Phil. 4:8).

Excellence in thought is urgently needed today, when scores are burdened with a punishing self-image, the evening news is saturated with stories of blood and tragedy, and video shops blatantly peddle mind-polluting pornography. In short, we're constantly bombarded with the opposite of the true, noble, right, pure, lovely, and admirable — those virtues that Paul admonishes us to meditate upon.

With the excellent One's help, we must and will swim upstream in our evil world, although the water is swift, treacherous, and polluted. We will intentionally fill our minds with his thoughts and purposes. Then our lives will take on revitalized meaning. Our perspectives will be healthy, positive, and hopeful. After all, we are "a chosen people, a royal priesthood, a holy nation, a people belonging to God … declar[ing] the praises of him who called [us] out of darkness into his wonderful light" (1 Peter 2:9).

It is not enough to have minds that radiate with his excellence. That same excellence must permeate our actions. We must be constantly involved in loving deeds.

Acting on Intentions

Someone said, "After all is said and done, there's a lot more said than done." After attaining to excellent thoughts, we must do what we know we must do.

What T. H. Huxley said about education is true concerning Christian excellence. To paraphrase: It motivates us to do what we should do, when it should be done, as it should be done, whether it is convenient or not.

The Epistle of James has a lot to say about the necessity of excellent deeds. The author poses a penetrating question: "What good is it, my brothers, if a man claims to have faith but has no deeds?" (2:14). His answer: "Faith by itself, if it is not accompanied by action, is dead" (2:17). "Show me your faith without deeds, and I will show you my faith by what I do" (2:18b). On a more somber note he warns, "Anyone, then, who knows the good he ought to do and doesn't do it, sins" (4:17).

In his checklist of things to be done by every true disciple of Christ, Peter instructs, "Make every effort to add to your faith goodness" (*arete*; 2 Peter 1:5). Why? "For if you do these things, you will never fall, and you will receive a rich welcome into the eternal kingdom of our Lord and Savior Jesus Christ" (1:10b-11).

Excellent deeds reflect the very nature and character of our excellent God. They're not optional for the Christian; they are standard. But what kinds of excellent deeds?

First, there are deeds of preparation. These are the actions that ready us for the ongoing, challenging race we must run against the forces of evil.

Ancient Olympians trained for a full year prior to the Games. Arduous discipline and abstinence characterized their lives during this critical period. Philostratus the Elder advised, "If you have worked hard enough to render yourself worthy of ... Olympia, if you have not been idle or ill-disciplined, then go with confidence; but those who have not trained in this fashion, let them go where they will."

The challenge for the Christian—which is like the challenge of a marathon—demands no less. Paul captures the spirit when he says, "I beat my body and make it my slave so that ... I myself will not be disqualified for the prize" (1 Cor. 9:27). Employing the same analogy, the writer to the Hebrews admonishes us to "throw off everything that hinders and the sin that so easily entangles, [so that we can] run with perseverance the race marked out for us" (12:1).

"Beat my body," "throw off everything that hinders"—these are bold words of action. They are words that imply discipline. However, it is a discipline grounded in love and hope, the kind possessed by America's late Olympic hero, Jesse Owens, who endured years of rigorous training to be victorious at the Berlin Games. His athletic excellence stunned the world, inciting racist spectator Adolf Hitler to storm out of the stadium in a rage. Was his accomplishment worth the sacrifice? Ask any patriotic American.

Our deeds of preparation for God's race must reflect deep dedication and intense love — the appropriate response to the One who offered (John 3:16) and continues to offer his best. But God makes our preparation satisfying, reminding us that we too will some day "have our Munich" as Satan witnesses our victory and his defeat!

But what about the race itself? **A second kind of good deed must emerge: deeds that serve others so that they will come to recognize God's love.** Robert Murray McCheyne said it well: "A Christian is [one whose deeds] make it easy for others to believe in God." What is implied? On one hand, our deeds must not offend. But our servantlike deeds must also intersect human need — in the name of the One who commanded us to give "cup[s] of cold water" (Matt. 10:42).

James provides a helpful list of examples:

persevere under trial (1:12)
be quick to listen and slow to anger (1:19)
refrain from showing favoritism (2:1)
care for the physical needs of others (2:15-18)
tame the tongue (3:7-8)
avoid fighting (4:1), adultery (4:4; i.e., "friendship with the world"),
    self-indulgence (5:5), grumbling against another, and swearing
    (5:12)
help those who have wandered from the truth (5:19-20)

These are running skills for the Christian marathoner who manifests excellence. They are fundamentals but are often neglected in our life.

How often I have neglected some of these essentials in the heat of my race! Continuing to hope for success, I've allowed opportunities to do excellent deeds to slip away. As a result, I've found myself doing such defeating things as jumping the gun (showing impatience), dropping the baton (betraying trust), pulling a hamstring (developing crippling guilt), and obeying the crowd (conforming). Have you ever succumbed to these temptations?

Failure in the Christian's race for excellence is serious. If we lose the mile run in the Olympics, none are impacted with eternal loss. But our mediocre deeds in life's race can seriously damage our witness to those who are desperately in need of our Savior.

If divinely endowed, self-giving, and unconditional *agape* love can give us loving thoughts and motivate us to do loving deeds, how can we attain it? How can we become incarnations of his love?

This One's by Invitation Only

An awareness of God's generous offer to provide us with an unlimited supply of love is important. However, it is not sufficient to bring it to pass. We must consciously choose to invite him into our lives. He comes by invitation. How do we go about inviting his excellence and gift of love?

First, we invite him through sincere confession. We must acknowledge past sins. After expressing a genuine sorrow, we must ask God to take them away (2 Cor. 7:10; Acts 17:30). This is followed by a promise to do an about-face — to begin the new life of love (2 Cor. 5:17; Eph. 4:22-24). Finally, we must accept by faith that we are forgiven (Rom. 10:9-10). Such faith is grounded on the promise of God's infallible Word. Thanks to the sacrifice of Jesus on the cross we know with assurance that "if we confess our sins, he is faithful and just and will forgive us our sins and purify us from all unrighteousness" (1 John 1:9).

When we have confessed in faith, the Holy Spirit confirms the truth of the experience in our hearts (Rom. 8:16-17). As a result, we know without doubt that we have been born again. We are pardoned rebels.

Second, at a subsequent time we invite him through complete consecration. This is a time when we surrender our will to his will. Such consecration is thorough and complete. It was what Paul wished for the Thessalonians when he declared, "May God himself, the God of peace, sanctify you through and through.

May your whole spirit, soul and body be kept blameless at the coming of our Lord Jesus Christ" (1 Thess. 5:23).[32]

Our heavenly Father has provided for this second work of grace, commonly referred to as entire sanctification.[33] In receiving this grace, our sinful nature is instantaneously cleansed.[34] Our original sin (in contrast to past sins that are

---

[32]One person suggested that "through and through" calls to mind the image of a piece of inlaid linoleum, whose color is the same from top to bottom. It is clear that in this verse, Paul is admonishing entire sanctification to those who had already confessed their sins and become born again. He continually thanks God for them (1:2); remembers their "work produced by faith," their "labor prompted by love," their "endurance inspired by hope" (1:3); refers to them as "brothers loved by God" who had been "chosen" (1:4), "imitators of us and of the Lord; in spite of severe suffering" (1:6), and "a model to all the believers in Macedonia and Achaia" (1:7). He declares that he thanks God because they "received the word of God" and "accepted it" fully (2:13). The Thessalonians were forgiven sinners! Nevertheless, the apostle beckons them to the second work of grace, namely, entire sanctification.

[33]Other terms for the consecration are *heart holiness, baptism of the Holy Spirit, second blessing, fullness of the Spirit. Entire sanctification* is this author's preference because it can be linked with initial sanctification, which takes place in confession. Both are sanctification. Both are works of the Holy Spirit. One focuses on the forgiveness of past sins; the other directs attention to the cleansing of our sinful nature. The so-called Holiness churches of our world boldly proclaim the doctrine of entire sanctification. They trace lineage to John Wesley, James Arminius, the Reformers, the church fathers, and biblical authors. It was John Wesley, however, who particularly popularized the teaching, making it the cornerstone doctrine of the Methodist church.

[34]According to J. Kenneth Grider, John Wesley and Holiness-movement writers teach that entire sanctification is instantaneous. Nevertheless, Wesley also perceived a gradual element in the second blessing as original sin is mortified. Some Holiness-movement writers employ progressive sanctification terms referring to a gradual preparation of the mind and heart for the all-at-once cleansing. Grider proceeds to offer five biblical bases for teaching that original sin is instantaneously cleansed in entire sanctification.

It is a baptism. John the Baptist proclaimed that Jesus would baptize with the Holy Spirit (Matt. 3:11). This occurred in the hearts of the disciples on the day of Pentecost. Then Christ's prayer, "sanctify them" (John 17:17), was answered. Their hearts were purified (Acts 15:9). Baptism occurs at a point in time. A person cannot be partially baptized and later fully baptized. Likewise, there is no gradual spiritual purification. Original sin is expelled, destroyed, cleansed at one stroke.

It is a sealing. Three times in the New Testament (2 Cor. 1:22; Eph. 1:13; 4:30) "sealing" is a symbol of entire sanctification. It suggests God's ownership and approval of our lives. And it suggests instantaneousness. A person could not keep on sealing a letter with hot wax.

forgiven in confession), which we inherited from Adam, is completely removed. We are purged of all uncleanness. More than pardoned rebels, we become intimate, obedient children of God — his transformed creation (Rom. 12:1-2).

When such a dramatic event takes place in our lives, important results are purity of heart (Acts 15:8-9) and power to witness (Acts 1:8).

In short, we are fully prepared for life's challenge. *Agape* love filters down into the deepest recesses of the heart. Not only are sin's symptoms removed (as with consecration), but the poisonous venom of evil is eradicated from the life's blood stream. The purity of divine love flows within. We have a clean bill of spiritual health!

In addition, we are empowered with a wisdom and boldness to effectively spread the Good News of Christ's love to others. Jesus realized this and thought about the need for his disciples to witness with excellence. After he had instituted the Lord's Supper, he fervently prayed to God for their complete conseration: "They are not of the world, even as I am not of it. Sanctify [Greek *hagiazo*, make holy] them by the truth; your word is truth. As you sent me into the world, I have sent them into the world. For them I sanctify myself, that they too may be truly sanctified" (John 17:16-19).

It is a circumcision. Circumcision is analogous to entire sanctification (see Col. 2:11, NASB). Paul is saying that the "body of the flesh" is circumcised. The state, condition, or principle of the flesh is cut away. And this, too, is not a more-and-more matter.

It is received by faith. If it were by works, then it would be gradual only, never becoming complete or fully obtained. But entire sanctification, like justification, comes by faith (Acts 15:8-9; 26:18). Although faith might suggest an extended quality, faith as the means of obtainment suggests that any consecrated believer may, at any instant, exercise the kind of believing trust which results in God's grace of entire sanctification.

The aorist tense. The verbal cognates of *hagiazo* (sanctify) suggest instantaneousness. The word, in its verbal forms, appears twenty-eight times in the New Testament. It is in the aorist tense twelve times, in the perfect tense seven times, and in the present tense nine times. The aorist tense, the most common one in the Greek, appears in numerous other words relating to entire sanctification. *Entire Sanctification: The Distinctive Doctrine of Wesleyanism* (Kansas City, MO: Beacon Hill, 1980), pp. 91-97.

Our Lord's prayer was no doubt answered on the day of Pentecost, when his disciples were filled with the Holy Spirit (Acts 2:1-4). They were sanctified holy and wholly (Acts 15:8-9) and readied for the mammoth task of evangelizing the world. They went forth with boldness (4:31). As a result, their world was turned right side up!

After confessing and consecrating, we are ready to invite God to help us with constancy. Having been purified, we must focus on Christian maturity. Consecration is like achieving the legal status of adulthood at age twenty-one. Suddenly privileges and rights—rights that we have never known before—become ours. Constancy, on the other hand, resembles the necessary growth that must take place throughout our adult life, through the good times and the bad.

In essence, Christian constancy means increasing in love, enlarging our capacity for God's love. Paul highlights constancy in his First Letter to the Thessalonians, when he says, "May the Lord make your love increase and overflow for each other and for everyone else, just as ours does for you" (3:12).

Love must grow and grow and grow in our hearts. We must do more than settle for consistency. Instead, we must constantly grasp for ever more of God's love. This can only bring about increasing glory for the One who is the source of all love.

Three invitations, but one guest: love. It is necessary for our personal salvation, for it alone opens the floodgates of God's presence. What's more, love is the ticket that allows us to enter wholeheartedly into the arena of effective witnessing.

Who could possibly refuse the universal offer to become authentic recipients of God's love/excellence? It is far brighter than any Olympic torch. Far more beautiful than the most intricate ancient Greek sculptures. Far more honorable than being a warrior in Alexander's victorious army.

And we can be engulfed in this glorious light of God's excellence without having to earn his favor (Eph. 2:8-9; Titus 3:5). Unlike the Greeks of old, who trembled for fear of Zeus' wrath for slight imperfections of conduct, we approach our God with confidence and trust (Heb. 4:16). We know all the while that he graciously offers to bestow his excellence to us as we will to do his will.

Biblical excellence is a glorious ideal for every Christian. It is a standard that activates our best energies and creativity, causing us to live our lives as he intended. Why? Because biblical excellence means divine love.

This is love observed in the excellencies of nature: brilliant tropical flowers in Hawaii, majestic geese in flight. This is love seen in excellent human expressions: Mother Teresa's sacrificial service, life-risking heroism at the site of a plane crash. But also it is love that makes us inwardly holy and at peace with the One who gives us ultimate fulfillment in our earthly existence—the One who promises us an inheritance in his eternal kingdom "that fadeth not away."

God is ready to assume full responsibility for the life wholly yielded to him. — Andrew Murray

Rather than giving God our ability, he wants our accessibility. — Earl G. Lee

Behold the turtle who makes progress only when he sticks his neck out. — Cecil Parker

5

Pursuing with Fervent Heart

The sound of some statements is like music to our ears. For example:

It's benign, not malignant.

All is forgiven.

It's a healthy baby.

The war is over!

We could all come up with our own list of statements that soothe our emotions, pour hope into our spirits, and bring deep comfort to our total beings.

But one statement should be near the top of all our lists: "Excellent job!" It means we have performed well. We have met, and even exceeded, the expectations of others—on a football field, in a classroom, or at the work place. We want our parents, employers, and peers to approve of our actions. When they assign the term *excellent* to what we've striven to do, we are pleased.

As followers of Christ, we yearn for his approval. We need to know that he considers us to be excellent, and to be doing things excellently, in our daily lives. Then, in that great day of judgment, we will hear him say the greatest words we will ever hear: "Well done, good and faithful servant! You have been faithful with a few things; I will put you in charge of many things. Come and share your master's happiness!" (Matt. 25:21).

But to know this fact is not enough. To realize that biblical excellence is divinely implanted *agape* love will not suffice. To comprehend the ways in which we invite that love into our life is insufficient.

The simple fact is that to know is not necessarily to do and be. People know that exceeding the speed limit costs lives, that smoking causes cancer, that gossip injures innocent people. But, in each of these cases and in so many more, awareness has failed to bring about needed change. In spite of education, intelligent Americans continue in self-destructive ways, consciously choosing to live foolishly and even flaunting their self-destructive behavior.

All of us have the problem of knowing more than we implement. We eat, drink, talk, work, play in excess. We neglect to write letters when we know we should, to fix a broken car, to rid ourselves of an arrogant attitude. We fail to follow through with putting what we know into practice.

We declare our reasons: "Not enough time." "Tried to improve before and failed." "It's not as bad as it seems." "Others get by, why not me?" "It's how I've always been." "God knows I'm human."

Don't misunderstand. Education is important. We need to become increasingly aware. To know that excellence/love is necessary and available is a crucial first step. But it is only a first step. We must be additionally motivated to action. Paul instructs the Philippians to "work out [their] salvation with fear and trembling" (Phil. 2:12). Similarly, Hebrews assures us that God "rewards those who earnestly seek him" (11:6). There is a need to engage the will in discipline. We need to act on what we know.

To have authentic Christian excellence, we must gear our-selves to follow the biblical admonitions discussed in the last chapter. We must prepare for change. We must anticipate, in faith, that we will be increasingly allowing our lives to respond to his love. Our attitude must be one of expectant readiness, motivated to march forward[35]

But are all motives pure? Is it not possible to be motivated to attain biblical excellence but for the wrong reasons?

God's Gift for My Glory

Satan tricks us into thinking we can attain *agape* love for our own benefit so the payoff package has our own name on it.

First, we're lured into believing that we are earning merit by our "bite-the-bullet" kind of obedience. As a result, we see ourselves as slaves, not sacraments. We submit to the yoke of painful duty in order to feel good about ourselves.

Second, Satan tempts us into the dangerous trap of legal-ism. This motivation finds ego satisfaction in doing what's necessary to be on God's list of very special people. The thought is: If I can be excellent/loving enough, he will have to give me prominence in his kingdom. James and John, along with their conniving mother, had a problem with this (Mark 10:35-45).

Third, the enemy of our souls would have us become excel-lent in order to outshine those around us. How easy it is to root our motivation for excellence in competition so that our real goal is winning for our own glory.

Fourth, we can develop a lopsided view of excellence. Attempting to love excellently in one area of our lives, we can neglect other important areas. In short, we can become imbal-anced and wobbly. In my survey, author John White was right in

---

[35]According to author Earl G. Lee, even spiritual "rest" is usually hard-earned. Hebrews states, "Let us labour therefore to enter into that rest" (4:11, KJV). Or, as the *Amplified Bible* admonishes, "Let us therefore be zealous and exert ourselves and strive diligently to enter into that rest [of God]." Once realized, this rest is not passive. It does not mean "being at ease." In Ps. 37:7, "rest" is taken from the Hebrew word that means "cease, be silent, submit in silence to what he ordains," in short, to be in a state of relaxed readiness to follow his guidance. Earl G. Lee, *The Cycle of Victorious Living* (Kansas City, MO: Beacon Hill, 1971), pp. 34-36.

saying that Christian excellence "is not so much a matter of being superior at some specific activity, as much as [it is] living an excellent, God-glorifying life."

Love must permeate all we do. Paul states, "So whether you eat or drink or whatever you do, do it all for the glory of God" (1 Cor. 10:31). A life of excellence penetrates and saturates every thought, attitude, and action so that, as the song declares, "Jesus [is] the Lord of all the kingdoms of [our] heart."

Finally, excellence must not be pursued because it leads to success. It is possible to choose Christian excellence over success, only to allow the desire for success to "come in the back door." For example, we might love in order to gain others' affections or possessions. Such love has little resemblance to authentic *agape* love.

Granted, success is often a derivative of inviting Jesus into our hearts, as our lives become disciplined and purposeful. John Wesley referred to this as the "love and lift" principle. If consecrated to God in faithful stewardship, and with a grateful heart, such success is not destructive — in fact, it is a blessing.

Nevertheless, more often it seems, success incapacitates. Why? Because it is perceived as life's panacea, and pursued relentlessly. Even when received as a derivative of our Christian walk, unless we are extremely vigilant, success can lead to spiritual paralysis.

With good reason, Charles Colson refers to the success gospel as "creeping greediness."[36] Cynthia R. Schaible in her insightful *Eternity* article further details the inherent dangers in the gospel of success:

> Excessively emphasizing the importance of a positive self-image, it ignores that we're worth little apart from Jesus (1 Cor. 2:2; Gal. 2:20).

> The doctrine provides the tragic illusion that there is enough room at the "success peak" for everyone. It teaches that all believers with enough "name-it-and-claim-it" faith can become elite in this world.

---

[36]Cynthia R. Schaible, "The Gospel of the Good Life," *Eternity*, February 1981, p. 21.

Rather than emphasizing the dynamic, revolutionary changes that take place in the life of the Christian, through our Lord, proponents of this attitude focus on the superficial changes that only alter some behavior patterns, specifically the ones that are necessary to "get you ahead."

The doctrine inflates God's promises so that they are made to include more than our needs (Matt. 6:8, 32).

It deflates God's blessings. They are perceived as related only to material things (Luke 12:22-23).

The success gospel allows no room for God's sovereign will, failing to recognize that sometimes God blesses, but more often, his blessings seem to mysteriously surface through suffering (1 Peter 4:12-14).

This sensually appealing but counterfeit doctrine promotes an inevitable lack of sensitivity to responsible stewardship and with it a denouncement of authentic servanthood.[37]

As Christians, we must realize that our excellence results in a far more valuable treasure than temporal success. In fact, our greatest glory comes when, in the face of severe tribulation, we can clutch the "torch of divine love" tighter. We realize that our full reward will come later (John 14:2-3). Furthermore, we know that we are pleasing Jesus during our earthly existence—and are assured of his constant care.

Having examined counterfeit motivations for pursuing Christian excellence, we once again remind ourselves of their fatal flaw: focusing attention on our own glory and profit.

Performing benevolent deeds is not enough. We can "speak in tongues of men and of angels," "prophe[sy]," "move mountains" (of difficulty), "give all [we] possess" and "surrender [our] bod[ies] to the flames" for the benefit of people (1 Cor. 13:1-3). But, in going to such extremes, we must determine whether we're doing such noble deeds for God's glory or for our own.

---

[37]Ibid, pp. 21-23, 26-27.

What is the best motive for attaining excellence in our life as a Christian? Put simply, it is seeking to glorify God.

Excellence Generated by an Altruistic Motive

Recall the last few words of the Lord's Prayer: "for Thine is the kingdom, and the power, and the glory forever. Amen." Truer words were never spoken. Our heavenly Father deserves all the glory forever. It follows that all biblical excellence that we possess, which is his gift in the first place, must be returned to him. In this way he is glorified and honored and we have realized our chief purpose in life.

Author Jerry Bridges summarizes this point well: "Christian excellence is the quality of life that results when a Christian seeks to live out every area of his life with the aim of pleasing ... and glorifying God. He is worthy of our most diligent efforts."

You may wonder: Doesn't Bridges have us reasonably comfortable, secure, and free Americans in mind? Glorifying God for his blessings is our natural response as Christians. But what about those who are harshly persecuted for their faith?

In his first epistle, Peter addressed such a people in the early church. These people lived in constant fear of oppression. The disciple Jesus called "the Rock" admonished them to be steadfast and even to rejoice in the midst of their trials, to be excellent in love in spite of all so that their faith would "glorify" God (1 Peter 2:12; 4:11, 16).

The motivation to glorify our Maker and his Son must be universal. In the same way that nature brings such glory to its Creator in so many beautiful and different ways, so we must also attain Christian excellence, in spite of our unique surroundings. Excellence for the glory of God!

If this is our sincere motivation, we will humbly and gratefully accept his timeless and trustworthy ways of teaching us about his excellence. These ways likewise bring glory to his name.

God's Lesson Plans

First, we learn from God's written Word. As we learned in chapter 4, our Bible confronts us with the importance of Christian excellence.

The apostle Paul, standard-bearer and embodiment of such excellence, admonishes, "I want you to be able always to recognize the highest and the best, and to live sincere and blameless lives until the day of Jesus Christ" (Phil. 1:10, *Phillips*). Another version states, "That ye may approve things that are excellent" (KJV).

John Stapert, editor of the *Church Herald*, offered a helpful explanation of this verse in his response to the survey. The Greek word for "what is excellent" can be translated "the things that differ." In short, as Christians, we must discern (v. 9) things that differ from being merely good. Ours must always be the highest and best. In another place, Paul instructed the Corinthian church to "covet earnestly the best gifts" (1 Cor. 12:31, KJV). In regard to the Greek word for "approve," Stapert suggested that it implies an investment of our total being rather than simply an intellectual consent.

This is an emphatic choice of words: "highest," "best," "approve," "a more excellent way." Such words are straightforward, direct, penetrating, and demanding, but necessary for our life to bring glory to God.

Second, God would have us learn from his incarnate Word, Jesus Christ. Christ is our model, our example, the incarnation of love-based excellence. Because of this, as Robert Murray McCheyne says, "For every [one] look [at ourselves, we should] take ten of Jesus Christ."

God's written lesson, as clear and helpful as it is, could not suffice. Our world needed a perfect embodiment of God's love. Our Lord is that embodiment. Because of him we have tangible hope. The early church realized this. As E. Stanley Jones said, they "did not say in dismay: 'Look what the world has come to,' but, in delight, 'Look what has come into the world!'" Today we share that same hope in Jesus Christ.

In our day it is easy to lose sight of the real Jesus and to picture a synthetic, counterfeit Lord who neatly conforms to our hedonistic cravings. Edward Kuhlman put it well:

Many speak of Jesus as if he were a character in a flat one-dimensional soap opera. Jesus comes with manicured nails and razorcut coiffure. He comes ... with teeth straight, white, and free of cavities. He comes as an Emmy winner with chest hair showing through the open shirt front, a gold chain encircling his tanned throat.

This is not the kind of excellence he possessed. Rather, Jesus was the supreme combatant of satanic power, described in Hebrews as the One who "learned obedience from what he suffered" (5:8), the "author and perfecter of our faith, who for the joy set before him endured the cross, scorning its shame" (12:2). We are invited to "consider him who endured such opposition from sinful men, so that [we] will not grow weary and lose heart" (12:3).

He was, by no means, a softy. Instead, he was engaged in a constant and agonizing fight against the powerful forces of evil. But through it all he remained excellent, loving the "unlovable."

Unlike others considered great in history, he provided a living example. He is more than a reference point in the past—One who taught valuable insights; One who exemplified what he taught. Our Savior died for our sins, the just for the unjust, so that we might be reconciled to God in our lifetime. But even more than this, he rose again to saturate us with his presence every moment (Gal 2:20)—to take the place of what we are. As W. Ian Thomas put it, "His *strength* for our *weakness*! His *wisdom* for our *folly*! His *drive* for our *drift*! His *grace* for our *greed* ! His *love* for our *lust*! His *peace* for our *problems*! His *plenty* for our *poverty*!" A living example.

So this is Christian excellence: divinely implanted *agape* love, undergirded by the right motive—the desire to bring glory to God. It is taught to us through the lessons he has provided: his written and incarnate Word.

But you may ask: What happens to the Christian excellence that is motivated by a desire to please him? Does God receive, and keep, all the glory for himself? Or are others blessed?

The Results of Excellence

In a word, God's glory continually recycles and recirculates, expanding all the while. Although our heavenly Father deserves, and greatly appreciates, all the glory we send his way, we ironically become beneficiaries. Those of us who lose ourselves in selflessly honoring him find ourselves blessed beyond measure (John 12:25). And we are blessed *because* we refuse to be excellent just to receive from God!

First, our world benefits when we glorify God through our excellence. We show others an example of the fulfilled life as the Father intends it to be lived. Our influence takes on a ripple effect as it impacts those who desperately need a reason to exist.

Technology has inundated our planet with gadgets and conveniences. As someone declared, it has made dentistry painless, bicycles chainless, carriages horseless, laws enforceless, cooking fireless, telegraphy wireless, coffee caffeineless, births weanless, oranges seedless, grass weedless, roads dustless, steel rustless, tennis courts sodless — and, in so doing, our lives godless.

Technology is not the real culprit. In fact, potentially, it can be employed to the glory of God and the advance of his Kingdom. Instead, it is people who are to blame. Godlessness often results when technological change distracts us from being dependent upon our Lord.

Our world needs people who excel in reflecting God's love more than it needs advanced technology. The Bible refers to such persons as the "aroma of Christ among those who are being saved and those who are perishing" (2 Cor. 2:15). A few verses later, they are termed a "letter from Christ" written "with the Spirit of the living God ... on tablets of human hearts" (3:3). Ephesians 2:10 likens us to "God's workmanship" or masterpiece that he exhibits to reflect his own excellence in a sin-sick world!

My survey posed the question: Why is Christian excellence so desperately needed in our world today? Some responses follow:

> Television has debilitated moral standards and reduced time spent in [reflecting on God]. — Kenneth Taylor

We have an incredible ethical crisis which threatens the disintegration of our world at an ever-accelerating rate. — Paul T. Culbertson

American society has gradually moved farther ... away from its Christian heritage. Consequently ... Christian values are being replaced by [those that are] humanistic. — Virginia Patterson

Because the world is suffering greatly from irresponsibility, mediocrity, and distorted values. — Howard A. White

All of these responses convey truth. Christian excellence is needed today. It has always been needed, but especially today when we have power to destroy our planet in minutes, when two-thirds of the people who have ever lived are presently living, when more than one billion are starving to death (ten thousand each day).

But what is even more crucial is that there are more opportunities for Christian witness than ever before! Wade Coggins, executive director of Evangelical Foreign Missions Association, spoke boldly: "We must demonstrate through Christian excellence that the gospel transforms and gives a new way of life. If our words are not backed up by such excellence we will lose the attention of the world, and fail to bring them to Christ."

Second, we as Christians reap bountifully when we glorify God through loving excellence. Not only is there a ripple effect, but there is also a boomerang effect. Paul declares, "And we, who with unveiled faces all reflect the Lord's glory, are being transformed into his likeness with ever-increasing glory, which comes from the Lord ..." (2 Cor. 3:18).

We are not glorifying ourselves, nor glorifying God in order to bring glory to ourselves. Rather, we are glorifying God! Then, as an unanticipated gift, we are increasingly showered with his blessing and glory. What a wonderful surprise God lovingly gives to us. But, when you really think about it, it is not so surprising after all. Our God always gives — and returns what we offer to him tenfold, a hundredfold!

Two Gifts in One

God helps us be more excellent in two ways. **First, through God's help, we grow in Christian excellence.** Perceiving life as a Christian vocation, we strive to develop our talents and maximize our strengths, becoming "a workman who does not need to be ashamed" (2 Tim. 2:15). But our excellence is Christian because we are motivated by the principle of love. We know that this brings glory to the excellent One.

In addition to receiving more Christian excellence, we progressively become more excellent Christians. After confession and consecration (see chap. 4), we focus our attention on constancy. Having received the gift of purity, we commit ourselves to maturity. Why? So that our witness will become more and more effective as we become increasingly Christlike. Ephesians 4:15 encapsulates this principle: "We will in all things grow up into him who is the Head, that is, Christ." Similarly, Peter instructs, "But grow in the grace and knowledge of our Lord and Savior Jesus Christ" (2 Peter 3:18).

This manifested excellence refines our Christian walk, enlarges our capacity for love, and allows that love to permeate all we are, say, and do.

This can and will take place as we "walk in the light, as he is in the light" (1 John 1:7). This same verse goes on to promise us that "the blood of Jesus, his Son, [keeps on purifying] us from every sin." God's spiritual filter system remains intact and operates to stop evil from dominating our life. In addition, that system expands in its capacity to generate *agape* love. The result is more glory for God—and a return of that glory to our world and life.

A Plan for Refurbishing

Renovation implies complete renewal from the ground up, but refurbishing means improvement of what exists. To refurbish our house is to do such things as paint the outside, update the landscaping, or add new shutters.

After being born again and sanctified wholly (spiritual renovation), we must adopt a plan for continual growth in Christian love (spiritual refurbishing). As is true of repairing a house, results cannot be expected overnight. Progressive excellence in the Christian life is just that, progressive. In fact, it is likely to seem regressive at times—taking a three-steps-forward-and-one-backward pattern. But it is the direction in which we are heading that is crucial.

Part 3 presents a plan for continual refurbishing. Each chapter presents a standard of excellence, based on God's Word, that will increase our capacity for (and refine our expression of) *agape* love. We need to apply each standard in ways that relate to our own life. The Holy Spirit graciously guides us as we do this, for he is our Counselor (John 14:16-17).

May our love-commitment deepen. May our giving glory to God increase. May our witness to a lost world become progressively effective. And may we be open to making the needed midcourse adjustments so that we may keep our eyes focused on following God.

Psalm 36:7 declares, "How excellent is thy loving kindness, O God!" (KJV). To comprehend this declaration fully is to desire this excellent, steadfast, divine love for ourselves—above everything! May that deep desire translate into a humble willingness to consider prayerfully his direction as we examine the principles of spiritual growth.

Part **3**

Excellence

Nurtured in Our Walk

It was not the outer grandeur of the Roman but the inner simplicity of the Christian that lived on through the ages. — Charles Lindbergh

God does not comfort us only to make us comfortable — rather He does it to make us comforters. — Navigator's *Daily Walk Bible*

If it is more blessed to give than to receive, then most of us are content to let the other fellow have the greater blessing. — Shailer Mathews

6

The Towel and the Cross

My friend and I were talking about what it means to be a true servant of Jesus Christ. He began to tell me a story. It centered around his father, who took pride in his skill at playing checkers. Not content to merely win, he would gleefully pulverize his opponents. After they were beaten, he would ridicule them until they were demolished in spirit. Family members and neighbors intensely disliked playing checkers with my friend's father. They considered it humiliating. Why should his insatiable ego be fed at their expense? They had a point.

But there was one who did fine playing this "Checkers Terminator." Who was it? My friend's mother. How did she survive his onslaught of arrogance? It was simple. While his goal was winning, hers was getting the game over as soon as possible. So her strategy was to give away her checkers quickly. An average game took seconds. His craving was satisfied — he won. But she was also delighted. Her giving had made him happy.

Our world is full of self-centered takers. Most live according to the strategy of my friend's father — winning, rubbing it in, thriving on competition while victories keep coming. Losing, or even having to share in victory, is considered unacceptable. Such persons live by the philosophy of the late football coach Vince Lombardi who declared, "Winning ... is the only thing!"

God offers us a contrasting standard. His idea is more like that of my friend's mother. He gave away all he had so that we might reap the benefits. And he keeps on giving to each of us every day. His was (and is) the excellence of unparalleled generosity. And so will be ours — if we grow in his kind of excellence. One word captures his brand of spontaneous, sacrificial giving — servanthood.

It's in the Book

God's Word repeatedly speaks about the idea of servanthood. The most common term for "servant" is *doulos*, which means "slave."[38] Not surprisingly, *doulos* was a title of humiliation in the ancient world. People frowned upon the idea of being subservient, of putting a master's interests before their own.

In contrast, the Bible describes the greatest biblical personalities as servants. Moses, the supreme lawgiver (Deut. 34:5); Joshua, the victorious commander (Josh. 24:29); David, the greatest of Israel's kings (Ps. 78:70); and the prophets (Isa. 20:3; Amos 3:7) were all described as the servants of God. In the New Testament, James (1:1), Jude (11), Paul (Rom. 1:1), and Peter (2 Peter 1:1) proudly claim the same title.

The idea of "servant" fits well with that of "lord" (*kurios*), meaning "absolute owner of a person or thing." *Kurios* was Paul's favorite title for Jesus, his Lord and Master. He realized that Jesus had lovingly died for his salvation. As a result, he no longer belonged to himself. He had been "bought at a price" (1 Cor.

---

[38]In 1 Cor. 4:1, Paul employs another term for "servant": *huperetes*. According to William Barclay, the term originally meant "a rower on the lower bank of a trireme, one of the slaves who pulled at the great sweeps which moved the triremes through the sea." It was pointed out that some commentators use this as a picture of Christ the pilot, who directs the course of the ship, and Paul as the servant accepting the orders of his Pilot, laboring only as his Master directs. William Barclay, *The Daily Study Bible: Letters to the Corinthians* (Philadelphia: Westminster, 1955), p. 40.

7:23). As Christ's slave, he became his master's herald (message-bearer), apostle (envoy or ambassador), and teacher (interpreter) (2 Tim. 1:11).

In addition, the New Testament uses the title *servant of Christ* for all Christians. "He who was a free man when he was called is Christ's slave" (1 Cor. 7:22b). Again, in Ephesians 6:6b, the apostle instructs us to live "like slaves of Christ, doing the will of God from [our] heart[s]."

But what, specifically, does it mean to grow in servanthood? William Barclay offers light. For him, growth in servanthood means becoming

> inalienably possessed by God,
> unqualifiedly at the disposal of God,
> unquestionably obedient to God,
> constantly in the service of God.[39]

Ownership, availability, obedience, and service. That's what it means to grow toward this crucial biblical ideal.

Greatness Redefined

As they trekked along the dusty road, James and John realized that the end was near. Jesus was on his way to Jerusalem for the final time. He had explained to them all that was to happen.

With the urging of their ambitious mother, the brothers decided to ask for positions of special prominence in Christ's kingdom. These were not simply positions of prominence; rather, they were *the* positions of prominence right next to their Lord.

To his naive disciples, Jesus announced a new standard of greatness:

> You know that those who are regarded as rulers of the Gentiles lord it over them, and their high officials exercise authority over them. Not so with you. Instead, whoever wants to become great among you must be your servant, and whoever wants to be first must be slave of all (Mark 10:42-44).

---

[39]William Barclay, *The Letters of James and Peter*, pp. 345-46.

Slave of all! Not vice presidents, but street sweepers, toilet cleaners, garbage men, people who are content with, and even grateful for, the dirty work. What a stinging rebuke to James and John, who had mistakenly assumed that Christ's kingdom is one of earthly pomp and splendor, and that greatness consists of place and position (i.e., success).

In essence, Jesus taught them (and us) that this world's idea of worth cannot be carried over into the spiritual realm. In Christ's kingdom, there is a complete reversal of earth's values. In heaven, gold is used to pave roads. Not the number of one's servants, but whom one serves, is the heavenly criterion for greatness. The final reward will be commensurate with the greatness of service humbly rendered.

Of course, Christ's own earthly ministry exemplified this principle: "For even the Son of Man did not come to be served, but to serve, and to give his life as a ransom for many." Again, in Luke 22:27 we read, "But I am among you as one who serves."

In serving, Christ became our supreme example. We are called upon to follow in his footsteps of servanthood. As someone said, he became what we are (man) to make us what he is (servant). That was why he picked up the towel (John 13:4) and soon thereafter the cross (Luke 23:25). Now it's our turn. For, as he declares in Matthew 10:24-25, "A student is not above his teacher, nor a servant above his master. It is enough for the student to be like his teacher, and the servant like his master."

Becoming his servant, and later sharing in his glory, sounds so inviting. What an honor to identify with our Lord and Master. If he considers servanthood essential, how can we settle for anything less!

Unfortunately, often our best intentions are not sufficient. We encounter unforeseen difficulties that make servanthood little more than an elusive dream. What are some of these?

Satan's Spoilers

The famous conductor Leonard Bernstein was once asked, "What is the most difficult instrument to play?" Without hesitation he replied, "Second fiddle." Then he explained, "I can get plenty of first violinists, but to find one who plays *second* violin with as much enthusiasm or *second* French horn or *second* flute, now that's a problem. And yet if no one plays second, we have no harmony."[40]

First, many Christians shy away from servanthood because, in reality, it means playing second fiddle, taking a back seat, going to the end of the line, relinquishing the credit, doing things in secret with no fanfare. The world advocates the opposite: toot your own horn, push ahead to the front of the line, demand credit, showcase your contributions.

Although sacrificing isn't difficult for me, sacrificing in secret is. That's probably why I give others a bad time about it.

Not long ago my mother heard a medical missionary tell about having to use razor blades instead of scalpels. Imagine a poor African lying on an operating table with the doctor cutting around his vital parts with razor blades. The very thought makes my skin crawl. Well, the heartstrings of my mom were plucked. She contributed a sum of money to purchase the scalpels.

It wasn't long before my philanthropist mother began telling me about all the positive reactions of others. Many people were giving her "strokes" for giving the money. Among themselves they were saying, "Did you hear? Mrs. Johnston gave a sizable sum to the missionary—even though she's on a fixed income." And Mom was savoring every delicious compliment.

"Mom," I said, "don't you know that your sacrificial gift is scoreless with God?" She asked, "Why do you say that?" "Because you've bragged to everyone. The Bible says that if we get the credit in this life, we certainly won't score points in heaven." She looked at me with a big grin and said, "I've given quite a bit in secret in the past. This time around I wanted to enjoy some of the reward in this life!" An honest answer to my teasing question.

Don't we all find it difficult to fade into the background after being benevolent? The "no-strings-attached" gift suddenly has plenty of strings, cords, and even ropes attached. What began as a secret, loving act of benevolence ends up being proclaimed from the rooftops (or in a testimony at church). Bernstein was right. It cuts against the grain of our nature to play second fiddle!

---

[40]Charles R. Swindoll, *Improving Your Serve: The Art of Unselfish Living* (Waco: Word, 1981), p. 34.

Second, while it's hard to play second fiddle, we find that it is easy to fake servanthood. Frauds are everywhere. Some obtain mail-order "doctorates" for twenty-five dollars. Others offer us "the deal of our lives"—which turns out to be swampland in Florida or a car that formerly belonged to someone like an Indy 500 speedster. In fact, I know a person who parks in the "handicap zone" and limps all the way into the store!

Some fakes are humorous. But one kind isn't funny at all. In fact, this pretender is pathetic. It is the person who feigns being a servant of Jesus Christ. Such an individual is being deceptive at the expense of God's kingdom, much like a foreign spy who claims allegiance to the "stars and stripes." He claims to represent something that, in reality, he strongly opposes.

Faking servanthood isn't difficult:

Give to big-name projects—favorites of those in power.

Advertise your generosity indirectly with exaggeration.

Develop the "look" of piety and sincerity.

Perform unimportant tasks—the jobs nobody wants—but in front of the "right" people.

God's Word rightly proclaims, "Man looks at the outward appearance ..." (1 Sam. 16:7). All people tend to give primacy to external countenance and thus are prone to misjudging. Christians, moreover, wanting to think the best of everyone, are especially vulnerable to the tactics of deceivers.

Realizing the vulnerability of God's community of believers, and seeing a rich payoff for being perceived as a servant, scores of individuals resort to the charade of servanthood. They go through the motions, use the right words and look the right ways at the right times. Sometimes we fool others and ourselves.

Third, some people are content to play second fiddle and even do it without the slightest trace of deceit, but in being a servant everything seems to backfire. Sometimes authentic servanthood isn't perceived as such. Instead, it is suspected, criticized, and even ridiculed. People ask, "Who's he trying to impress?" One survey respondent rightly declared, "We [often] see pacesetters as troublemakers [who show us up] by comparison." People who set the pace with sacrifice are resented the most because they produce guilt in those who realize their own shortcomings.

Then there are well-intentioned servants who use the wrong methods. They are enthusiastic, courageous, sincere, but a bit impulsive and unwise.

Peter was such a person. It was the week before the crucifixion. He boldly proclaimed to our Lord that he would never forsake him (Matt. 26:33). Soon thereafter, this "Rock" walked with Jesus to Gethsemane. In a rapid succession of events, the man of many promises twice went to sleep while Jesus prayed; cut off the ear of a soldier who had reached out to seize the Savior; three times denied that he was a follower of (or even knew) the Master; wept bitterly at his failures (Matt. 26:75).

Peter, I know you better than you think. I've risen from my knees after a time of close communion and inspiration, intending to be completely servantlike in everything that was to happen that day. But then, when the real test came, I brought only disappointment to the God I serve. Inwardly I could only weep bitterly.

Pressures — the flat tire, the undeserved insult, the hard, efficient work that goes unrecognized — have a way of spoiling our plans. All of a sudden attitudes emerge that choke the Spirit of Christ. Like Peter, we go to sleep (retreat from responsibility), cut off some poor man's ear (become aggressive), deny our Lord (seize control of our lives), and end up demolished in spirit.

But is such a chain of events inevitable? Are we destined to failure? Is true New Testament servanthood beyond our reach? Not at all. We can look around and see persons who become better servants with every passing day. They warm our hearts and give us hope.

What seem to be the characteristics of such persons? By examining this question, perhaps we can obtain some needed direction of our own lives.

Applying the Formula of Servanthood

Most people can probably agree with much that has been said in this chapter. The need for attaining love/excellence in our servanthood is evident. And, yes, there are definite barriers along the way.

But what about becoming more servantlike with each passing day? Are there fundamentals that we must master? If so, what are they?

First, we must be prepared to accept inconvenient interruptions and to accept them as providential gifts from God. How often we squeeze God and his work into our busy schedule. As an inevitable result, he is shortchanged as are we. There's the five-minute "good-morning—good-bye" time in the morning, the "wait-'til-nobody's-looking" blitz prayer at mealtime, the "not-now-I'm-too-busy" response to a request for service.

When we are true slaves of our heavenly Father, his timing will be our timing—even if it means losing track of time. Jesus often did. Neither he nor anyone else wondered about time when he was astounding the scholars in the temple at age twelve. And how about the time that he taught on the mountain? Everyone's attention remained riveted on him, even though their stomachs were growling with hunger. They became so hungry that he had to perform a miracle in order to feed them!

Desiring to be more servantlike, we must increasingly involve our best energies in worshipping him and helping his children in need, when they are in need. Have you noticed? Needs and crises refuse to conform to our timing. In fact, they seem to sabotage our schedules. Consider our Lord's parable of the Good Samaritan. This fellow was severely inconvenienced. His schedule was torn to shreds. He handed over his travel money to a strange hotel manager for someone he didn't even know. Yet he was not deprived of the joy of being inconvenienced for God.

You might think that in those times, people didn't have all that much to do. How about today? Are there really any busy persons who drop everything to care for someone in need? Do you know of any? I do.

He doesn't know I know. In fact, that was the whole idea. He didn't want anyone to know. He was a presiding officer in the denomination to which I belong. If anyone has a more demanding schedule, I don't know who it was.

It was the big day of dedication for a beautiful new church building in Dallas. The crowd gathered. There was only one problem. The speaker was uncharacteristically late. What had happened? People began to worry. Some even panicked—not unlike church people on such occasions. Finally, the speaker arrived to perform his duties and apologized for being tardy. The service ended and everyone went home.

It wasn't until the next week that the church learned the real story. A woman called the church office. Her story was beautiful. She had experienced severe car trouble on the busiest freeway in Dallas. Cars raced by. After what seemed like an eternity, one car stopped and backed up to where she was standing.

She was at wit's end, exhausted, disgusted, even angry. The tall stranger spoke calm words of comfort. Then he took her to get assistance at a time when almost everything was closed. Finally, he found help to repair her car. Only then did the Good Samaritan disappear. She called the church to express gratitude.

Inconvenienced? Certainly he was, and ever concerned about his obligation to the church. But that didn't keep him from stopping. We too must be willing to interrupt our schedules to assist someone in need. This is the first principle of servanthood. But how do we know when someone is in need?

Second, enhanced servanthood means increased spiritual sensitivity to (and awareness of) others. This means turning away from ourselves and toward others. It means having invisible radar that is constantly scanning to locate those who are hurting, those for whom our Master deeply cares.

Most of us are absorbed by thoughts of personal well-being. Every situation, circumstance, person, and object is judged according to how it will better or worsen our life. No wonder we use personal pronouns so often and constantly bore others with inconsequential trivia about our own existence.

I worked in a bottle factory to put myself through college. It amazed me how my fellow workers used one another as listening boards. There was rarely give-and-take communication. Rather it was: "You're my captive audience. Now you listen to what is important in my life. I demand it."

To cite an example, I overheard two women talking. One took out a miniature picture album and made the other listen to every detail of her family history. But the other woman didn't remain passive. She would break in whenever her friend took a breath and talk about *her* family — never referring to anything the first woman had said. Neither listened to the other.

As servants of Jesus Christ, we must break out of our self-orbits. Our jobs, possessions, security, family must become secondary. "And we ought to lay down our lives for our brothers" (1 John 3:16b). I do not take this to mean martyrdom, although it could also refer to that. Rather, it seems as though the reference is to investing our lives in the lives of others, especially those who are in need. Verse 17 goes on to say, "If anyone has material possessions and sees his brother in need but has no pity on him, how can the love of God be in him?"

Satan distracts us from bearing the burdens of others. A hardening effect sets in. We're used to seeing people killed on television. We drive through dilapidated ghettos without the slightest sense of compassion. Then, when another shares an earnest, desperate need, we yawn and say to ourselves, "You've got your problems and I've got mine."

God wants to sensitize us to the hurt he feels when he sees human suffering. Being his servant means accepting his heartbreak, deeply caring for others' pain and suffering, and doing something about it.

Finally, becoming more servantlike means looking to God alone for reward. We should not anticipate the applause of the ones we have helped — be they strangers, friends, or even family members!

Servanthood is so special because it is done for God and is rewarded by God. In Christ's Sermon on the Mount, he explains that our heavenly Father sees our piety, giving, and prayers done in secrecy. Then he responds by rewarding us openly (Matt. 6:1-6, KJV).

One thing has always been hard for me to understand. After accepting inconvenience, becoming sensitive to another's need, and even responding sacrificially to that need, I've noticed that the persons I've helped often seem to resent me thereafter. Perhaps the recipient of my benevolence feels embarrassed that he needed assistance, since our society praises self-sufficiency and condemns dependency. Or maybe he fears that I'll expect an outpouring of gratitude as my payment. All I know is that often a barrier arises between me and the person I've assisted, even when it has been a "let's-never-talk-about-it-again" situation. Perhaps the best approach is complete anonymity.

Helping is a spontaneous act, as natural as breathing, for his servants. Its focus must be on bringing glory to his name. In addition to rewarding us later in heaven, he never fails to reward our inner spirit. We are given a deep inner peace and assurance and an abiding sense of his approval—the greatest gift of all!

Silent, Secret Service

Will we become increasingly servantlike? We must! Will it be rewarding? Immensely! For servanthood is a giant step toward Christian excellence.

Ruth Harms Calkin has written a poem entitled "I Wonder." Desiring to follow our Lord's example, we will answer a resounding *yes* to its closing question!

> *You know, Lord, how I serve You*
> *With great emotional fervor*
> *In the limelight.*
> *You know how eagerly I speak for You*
> *At a women's club.*
> *You know how I effervesce when I promote*
> *A fellowship group.*
> *You know my genuine enthusiasm*
> *At a Bible study.*
>
> *But how would I react, I wonder*
> *If You pointed to a basin of water*
> *And asked me to wash the calloused feet*
> *Of a bent and wrinkled old woman*
> *Day after day*
> *Month after month*
> *In a room where nobody saw*
> *And nobody knew.*[41]

---

[41]Source unknown.

The older I grow, the more clearly I perceive the dignity and winning beauty of simplicity in thought, conduct, and speech: a desire to simplify all that is complicated and to treat everything with the greatest of naturalness and clarity. — Pope John XXIII

The gospel can be condensed into these simple words: "Jesus loves me this I know, for the Bible tells me so." — Karl Barth

This world has enough for everyone's need, but not enough for everyone's greed. — Mahatma Gandhi

Civilization is a limitless multiplication of unnecessary necessities. — Mark Twain

7

Lowly, But Not Losers

Figure 1
To Queue If All Lines Are Busy
• You Will Hear a Callback Announcement
• Depress 5
• System Will Announce a Three-Digit Queue Number
• Hang Up Handset
• You Will Receive Three Short Rings When a Line Is Available
• Lift Handset
• System Will Repeat Three-Digit Queue Number
• Call Is Placed

The instructions in Figure 1 are not those for launching a rocket from Cape Canaveral. They come from an instruction sheet on my desk.

At the university where I teach, we recently installed a four-million-dollar, computerized, twenty-first-century IBX telephone system. It does everything but boil water and scratch your back. It has enough complicated options to give Ma Bell a migraine headache.

To name a few, you can place and retrieve a call on hold while entertaining the waiting party with recorded music, set up a seven-way conference, program into the computer for automatic dialing, leave an electronic message if there is no answer, or add parties to an existing call.

There's only one problem. The system is so complex that, in spite of an extensive seminar, few people have learned to use it effectively. When it is used incorrectly, the result is frustration: eardrum-splitting static and whistles, or reprimands from the annoyed party who receive repeated "wrong number" calls. People are able to read the names of the "intruders" on the digital screen. I sometimes long for the simplicity of the old-fashioned, two-party crank phone. I'm sure it would make me less cranky!

We all have areas of our lives that we want to simplify. There are the "self-cleaning" ovens that won't, the "maintenance-free" car batteries that aren't, and the "self-propelled" lawnmower that doesn't. To repair them requires the knowledge of a mechanical engineer. And how about those new, revolutionary filing systems which permanently lose valuable papers? It takes a photographic memory to remember the subject categories!

But this relates to things. What about relationships with people? Ask a Pentagon employee about the staggering complexity of any operation. Or, volunteer to serve on a committee. (Someone defined a committee as the unable, appointed by the unwilling, to do the unnecessary.)

Better yet, carefully listen to the sermon of a minister who tries to impress with his vocabulary. You're apt to hear words that make you dizzy—like "supralapsarianism" and "premillennialism." (One exasperated layman was overheard declaring, "Six days a week our pastor is invisible; then, on the seventh, he's unintelligible!")

We need simplicity in all areas of life, especially our Christian walk. The Bible calls us back to God's basics, inviting us to discover (or rediscover) those simple essentials that can give our lives abundant meaning and maximum fulfillment. Let's carefully examine the timeless and valuable message of simplicity.

The Bible: Advocate of Simplicity

Our world honors success, temporal security, and status — goals that often complicate life. Furthermore, "experts" can't seem to agree on the means of attaining these goals. As someone remarked, "If you lined up all the world's experts, end to end, they'd never reach a conclusion."

Biblical writers, on the other hand, spotlight simplicity. The psalmist explains that the simple are revived and made wise by God's law (19:7). Also, they freely receive his generous protection (116:6). Paul instructs the Romans (12:8, KJV) to give with simplicity. To the church at Corinth he states that he has dealt with it "in simplicity and godly sincerity, not with fleshly wisdom, but by the grace of God" (2 Cor. 1:12, KJV).[42] Finally, he expresses fear that Satan might deceive its members, "so [their] minds [will] be corrupted from the simplicity that is in Christ" (2 Cor. 11:3, KJV).[43]

But what exactly does God's Word mean when it refers to being simple? What key themes emerge from this important concept?

First, God chooses the weak and lowly rather than those who connive to gain power. Lowly persons are described in Christ's Beatitudes — the "poor in spirit," "those who mourn," "the meek," "those who hunger and thirst for righteousness," "the merciful," "the pure in heart," "the peacemakers," and "those who are persecuted because of righteousness" (Matt. 5:3-10).

Paul informed the Corinthians that they weren't nearly as great as they thought they were. In addition, he said that for his most crucial assignments God often uses people thought to be insignificant. In the apostle's words, "God chose the foolish things of the world to shame the wise ... the weak things ... to

---

[42]*Phillips* translation of 2 Cor. 1:12: "Our dealings with you, ... have been absolutely aboveboard and sincere before God. They have not been marked by any worldly wisdom, but by the grace of God."

[43]*Phillips* translation of 2 Cor. 11:3: "I am afraid that your minds may be seduced from a single-hearted devotion to him by the same subtle means that the serpent used toward Eve."

shame the strong ... the lowly ... and the despised things ... so that no one may boast before him" (1 Cor. 1:27-29).

We are inclined to think God chooses "big names" to do important jobs. So we showcase celebrities who are Christians: baseball stars, politicians, beauty queens, millionaires. The Corinthians thought the same way. But Paul disagreed. He knew that our heavenly Father uses seemingly insignificant people. His key point: It's our weakness God wants, more than our strength; our accessibility, more than our ability.

But didn't Paul have impressive credentials? Not really. He admits to not being much of a preacher — "preach[ing] the gospel — not with words of human wisdom, lest the cross of Christ be emptied of its power" (1 Cor. 1:17).

Paul's critics went even further, saying that "in person he is unimpressive and his speaking amounts to nothing" (2 Cor. 10:10). *The Acts of Paul and Thecla* (a third-century apocryphal writing) describes his appearance: "low stature, bald, crooked thighs, handsome legs, hollow eyed ... with a crooked nose."[44]

In addition, Paul had a serious defect which he described as a "thorn in the flesh" and which God refused to take away. In the words of his divine Master, "My power is made perfect in weakness" (2 Cor. 12:9). Paul's weakness allowed God's power to flow through him better, so that he could proclaim, "For when I am weak, then I am strong" (2 Cor. 12:10).

Paul didn't boast of his graduate degrees, but of his weakness: poverty, beatings, stoning, shipwrecks, imprisonments. He declared, "If I must boast, I will boast of the things that show my weakness" (2 Cor. 11:30).[45]

What is true concerning Paul is true about so many others in God's Word. Old Testament leaders were weakness personified! When God asked Moses to lead the children of Israel, Moses claimed that he wasn't good enough (Exod. 3:11), lacked credibility (4:1), and lacked eloquence (4:10). Others who were chosen by God responded initially in a similar manner:

---

[44]William Stewart McBirnie, *The Search for the Twelve Apostles* (Wheaton: Tyndale House, 1982), p. 291.

[45]John F. Alexander, "Weakness: An Entryway for God," *Other Side*, September 1983, pp. 8-9.

Gideon: "My clan is the weakest in Manasseh, and I am the least in my family" (Judg. 6:15).

Saul: "But am I not a Benjamite, from the smallest tribe of Israel, and is not my clan the least of all the clans of the tribe of Benjamin?" (1 Sam. 9:21).

David: "Who am I, and what is my family or my father's clan in Israel ...?" (1 Sam. 18:18). "I'm only a poor man and little known" (18:23). "Whom are you pursuing? A dead dog? A flea?" (24:14).

Solomon: "But I am only a little child and do not know how to carry out my duties" (1 Kings 3:7).

Amos: "I was neither a prophet nor a prophet's son, but I was a shepherd, and I also took care of sycamore-fig trees" (Amos 7:14).

Gayle D. Erwin graphically describes our Lord's disciples, whom he terms "a motley crew":

> [Jesus] went to the streets and wharves and picked out the strangest crew ever to be sent out on a mission to change the world. Had you been walking within fifty feet of them you probably would have detected the odor of fish.
> He had a Zealot and a tax collector on the team which is a combination not unlike a Black revolutionary and a Ku Klux Klan member. Some of them had heavily identifiable accents inappropriate to the need for eloquence on the team. He was found constantly among the sordid—from the violent to the crafty to the sensual.[46]

God chose (and still chooses) those convinced of their own dependency on him to confound the proud and powerful; the weak of the world to confound the wise. He inspired his prophet, Ezekiel, to declare, "All the trees of the field will know that I the LORD bring down the tall tree and make the low tree grow tall" (Ezek. 17:24). Truly, it is the "meek" (the humble; those who

---

[46]Gayle D. Erwin, *The Jesus Style* (Palm Springs, CA: Ronald N. Haynes Publishers, 1983), pp. 18-20.

manifest a lowly spirit) who will inherit the earth. These, along with Zechariah, know that it is "not by might, nor by power, but by [God's] Spirit" (Zech. 4:6, KJV). A total reliance upon that Spirit yields a God-honored simplicity.

Second, God honors sacrifice more than affluence. Our lives become complicated when we acquire gadgets and luxuries. A considerable amount of time and energy is required to locate, pay for, and maintain such items. Also, people become confused, asking themselves whether we are committed to God or to our possessions.

I've always been impressed by the "loose grasp" John Wesley had on things. It wasn't that he made little money. He earned more than most people of eighteenth-century England. Rather, his secret is contained in his philosophy of money: "Money and I have never been the closest of friends. The truth is, we are scarcely passing acquaintances. I've always made it a practice to make all I can to save all I can to give all I can."[47] And give he did—to the education of ministers, construction of churches, betterment of the poor. He refused to raise his standard of living, so that each increase in salary meant more money for God's kingdom.

How much is it possible to live without? The families of one church decided to experiment, living on an average budget of a Third-World family. They planned to do this for one month. Drastic measures were called for: walking and riding bicycles instead of using the car, extending food supplies by using plenty of carbohydrates (e.g., pasta) instead of meats, unplugging appliances and using candles rather than lights. The results were devastating.

Bickering ensued as individuals battled for their fair share. Many began to cheat, sneaking more than the rules allowed. Some had severe health problems. As a result, the experiment had to be discontinued after two weeks. Even in this limited way, identification with the Third World's plight could not be realized.

Perhaps it should not be realized. Little is gained by being subjected to such destitution, especially when you're not used to

---

[47]This quote is transcribed from a taped performance of D. Paul Thomas, who dramatized Wesley's life in a play entitled *A Heart Strangely Warmed.*

its dangerous effects. Also, being comfortable and modestly sustained is not necessarily sinful. It is possible to overstate the case against having physical resources.

As a carpenter, Jesus was probably from the middle class of Galilee. Although he was often among the poor, he frequently interacted with those with considerable means. He dined at the banquet tables of wealthy Pharisees (Luke 7:36). Joseph of Arimathea (Matt. 27:57) and Nicodemus (John 19:39), who became disciples of our Lord, were wealthy.

By no means was Jesus a rigid ascetic. His enemies accused him of being a glutton and drunkard (Luke 7:34)—a malicious, exaggerated charge. Yet, he did enjoy joyous celebrations like a wedding festival (John 2:1-2). He allowed perfume which was worth a year's wages to be poured over his head and feet while the disciples grumbled about the needs of the poor (Matt. 26:6-12).

Nevertheless, acceptance of such persons and circumstances does not mean that our Lord failed to see the dangers of wealth. His parable of the rich farmer pointed to the dangers of hoarding. Jesus called the farmer a "fool" (Luke 12:16-21). The Master waged war against the materialism of his day by declaring, "Watch out! Be on your guard against all kinds of greed; a man's life does not consist in the abundance of his possessions" (Luke 12:15). He also said, "You cannot serve God and mammon" (Matt. 6:24, KJV). Wealth is a rival god![48]

Our Lord's teaching is clear. Without trying to call attention to ourselves, we must live simply. Amassing a fortune in order to hoard and gloat, and in spite of global starvation, is not a worthy life ambition. It deprives the desperate others with whom we must share.[49] Also, it shows the world wherein our security lies. It builds walls, rather than bridges, between ourselves and the

---

[48]Richard J. Foster, *Freedom of Simplicity* (San Francisco: Harper and Row, 1981), pp. 40, 42.

[49]What good would result if Christians shared even 10 percent more than they do currently. Christians worldwide annually earn 6.5 trillion dollars and own two-thirds of this planet's resources. Their average income is $4,500 per year, three times that of non-Christians. But, there are more than two hundred million Christians in the grip of poverty. Increased generosity on our part would help these as well as non-Christians who suffer so greatly. (Statistics are from the *World Christian Almanac*.)

less affluent. How much better is it to follow the widow's example and make our giving to God truly sacrificial (Mark 12:42-43), and, as Paul adds, to do so cheerfully (2 Cor. 9:7).

Third, we honor our heavenly Father more when we offer sincere thanksgiving than when we make constant demands. The other day my friend, Inez, approached me with a big smile and said, "I've had this unbelievable problem for the last year. It has caused me anguish." I asked the question she seemed eager to answer: "Why do you look so happy and peaceful now?" Her reply: "Because I finally decided to quit nagging God and start thanking him. And that has made all the difference in the world!"

David tells us to "delight [ourselves] in the Lord and he will give [us] the desires of [our] heart" (Ps. 37:4). And when we do purposely delight, it is miraculous how God transforms our desires. We begin wanting most what we most need: his presence in our life. Our genuine thankfulness allows him to generously fill us with that presence.

Paul tells us to "rejoice in the Lord always." To emphasize the point he adds, "I will say it again: Rejoice!" (Phil. 4:4). We ask Paul, "What about the times we're under severe stress?" He declares, "Do not be anxious about anything, but in everything, by prayer and petition, with thanksgiving, present your requests to God" (v. 6). We reply, "Yes—yes—don't keep us in suspense. If we do this, what can we expect?" Again Paul furnishes the answer: "And the peace of God, which transcends all under-standing, will guard your hearts and your minds in Christ Jesus" (v. 7).[50]

Begging, pleading, and coaxing God to respond to our laundry list of requests makes prayer complex. When we do so, we visualize him as reluctant to help. As a result, we find ourselves groping for enough convincing arguments, impressive words, and biblical promises to change his attitude toward our plight.

Such an approach is not one of simple faith. Paul urges us to have simple faith when he reminds us that we are sons of God, inhabited by the Spirit of his Son. As his sons, we must relate to

---

[50]Earl G. Lee, *The Cycle of Victorious Living* (Kansas City, MO: Beacon Hill, 1971), pp. 28-33. Lee seems to equate "purposeful delight" with thanksgiving. He employs an acrostic to explain the meaning of delight: Daily Everything Laid Into God's Hands Triumphantly.

him as our loving Father (Gal. 4:5-7; Rom. 8:15; the word *Abba* means "daddy" in today's parlance). That is why the writer to the Hebrews says, "Let us then approach the throne of grace with confidence, so that we may receive mercy and find grace to help us in our time of need" (4:16). We know that he is more eager and willing to respond than even our own earthly father (Matt. 7:11; Luke 11:13).

Offering thanksgiving is a supreme act of worship. Demanding, accompanied by a spirit of doubt, is an act of desperation, a desperation that makes everything seem too complex and confusing.

However, the heartfelt expression of thanksgiving is not limited to words. The scene is the Boston shoreline. An event occurs, without fail, each day at about the same time. An old man appears carrying a bucket full of fresh shrimp. The seagulls are quick to spot their friend and flock to his feet. Some are bold enough to hop on his shoulders. A wide grin breaks out on his face as he feeds them all the shrimp. They thoroughly enjoy a connoisseur seagull's delight!

People used to observe the daily ritual in amazement. Many shook their heads in disgust and thought: What a shame to waste expensive shrimp on the birds! But that was before they learned this story.

The man had been a famous admiral of the American forces in World War II. The Germans torpedoed and sunk his ship, but he and a few of his men managed to climb into a lifeboat. In that cramped vessel they floated for many days, enduring the scorching sun, storms, and a scarcity of food. The men began to die, one by one, until only a few remained, including the admiral. Then came the day that he became dizzy and collapsed. Starvation was near. But while he was lying there, his glassy eyes focused on a small white object next to him. It was a seagull. And it didn't move. His weak and trembling hand slowly reached out and took hold of the gull's foot. It was to become his "manna from heaven," providing enough nourishment to remain alive a few more hours. But that was just long enough to sight an island, where he found safety.

Today, people no longer blame the admiral for providing an expensive banquet for Boston's seagulls. Now they understand.

His is a simple act of humble gratitude. Every piece of shrimp offered says "thank you" to God and his feathered friends.

But the admiral's thankful spirit was born of adversity. Is it possible to be thankful in the midst of abundance? I once heard a Thanksgiving Day speaker say, "All that's necessary for us to be unthankful is to have what we need." True indeed. At such times we are tempted even to nag God for luxuries.

It is time to cease clamoring and begin daily thanking—for big blessings, for small ones, in big ways, but also in small ways—like the admiral.

The biblical way of simplicity yields Christian excellence. How can we find that way? We need to acknowledge our weakness, become truly sacrificial, and remember to be genuinely thankful.

But how does this three-part biblical admonition translate into our individual Christian life? Is there a set pattern we should follow?

Different Steps to the Same Drummer

While I was Dean of Students at a small Christian school in Ohio, I visited a nearby Amish community. I was struck by the sameness. There was simplicity, but it was the carbon-copy kind. All the houses were white with look-alike furniture and blue curtains. Every man wore a beard and dressed in black with a wide-brim hat. Each woman donned a bonnet, shawl apron, and *halsduch* (kerchief). And everyone was transported in the same style black buggy pulled by horses. While respecting their sincerity, I came away questioning their wisdom in forcing everyone into the same mold.

Our God created rich diversity throughout his glorious creation. Like the flowers, birds, and snowflakes, we are all created differently in gifts, temperaments, and talents. Our God desires to tailor-make his grace to fit our unique existence so that we can increasingly realize our full potential as we are and where we are. Simplicity is, indeed, our biblical ideal, but not the kind which demands rubber-stamp uniformity. What is simple to one may be complex to another. Nevertheless, some suggestions might be helpful, provided we prayerfully adapt them to our unique circumstances. The suggestions fit into two categories: internal and external simplicity.

Internal Simplicity

Find time each day to humbly meditate upon God's Word and seek his guidance in fervent prayer.

Fast at least once each week, without telling others. Use the money for a good cause and the time for meditation.

Periodically make a thank-you list to God, enumerating recent blessings, whether they be great or small. Construct another list of requests that, by faith, you believe God is responding to.

Read one good Christian book each week. Balance your reading list with books that challenge as well as books that comfort.

Write something in your spiritual diary each day. It can be in the form of a letter to God.

Practice the presence of Christ. Imagine that Jesus is by your side throughout the day. Begin with one hour, then gradually increase your time of awareness.

Ask a trusted Christian friend to tell you of your faults in a spirit of Christian love. Reject the temptation to be defensive or discouraged. Realize that God offers to be your partner in improvement.

Cultivate the ability to truly worship every moment you are in a worship service. Fervent prayer, concentrating on the words of songs, and taking notes on sermons can be helpful.

Memorize key passages in God's Word or the words of inspirational hymns.

Strive to glean a spiritual lesson out of situations that occur in the course of a day (e.g., at the laundromat concentrate on the importance of "washing" in the Scriptures).

External Simplicity

As often as God leads, give away something to which you are strongly attached. Preferably, you should give anonymously to someone in need.

Give a faith gift (beyond your means) to God's kingdom, whether it be to a church, Christian college, or missionary cause. Promise God that amount when (not if) he provides it—believing that he will.

Continually suggest ways that your church can be less "building and facility conscious" and be more "people conscious." If people do not respond, dare to reapportion your church giving as an example.

Refuse to purchase gaudy luxuries for the sake of being "seen of men." Do not reject buying quality items, but reject fads and overpriced brands.

Plan to use cars, clothing, and appliances for a longer period of time. Much that is thought to be out of date is perfectly usable.

Do more bicycle riding and walking. It is healthy and sets an example for being a good steward of God's resources.

Minimize your reliance upon costly, empty-caloried junk food. Also, in regards to meat, favor that which swims (fish) and has wings (chicken). Reasons: health and cost.

Dedicate one "big-gift" day (e.g., birthday, Christmas) to others in need. Instead of exchanging with another, or receiving many presents from others, request that others give to a needy cause.

Make it known to all family members that you are willing a substantial portion of your estate to God's kingdom. Explain the reasons.

Periodically give up comforts for a span of time (e.g., air conditioning, television, eating out, customary vacations).

The prayerful cultivation of simplicity is every Christian's business. And as simplicity is increasingly practiced, its untold value is increasingly evident. May we apply its principles to our life, as we seek to travel a more excellent journey. These principles are reflected in an inspiring poem by William Ellery Channing:

My Symphony

I will seek elegance rather than luxury,
refinement rather than fashion.

I will seek to be worthy more than respectable,
wealthy and not rich.

I will study hard, think quietly,
talk gently, act frankly.

I will listen to stars and birds,
babes and sages, with an open heart.

I will bear all things cheerfully, do all things
bravely, await occasions and hurry never.

In a word I will let the spiritual, unbidden
and unconscious grow up through the common.[51]

---

[51]The poem is transcribed from a taped sermon of the Reverend Lamar Kincaid, who spoke at Longboat Key Chapel, Longboat Key, Florida, in 1973.

Keep yourself clean and bright, for you are the window through which you must see the world. — George Bernard Shaw

Who will tell you the truth? An enemy who hates you bitterly, and a friend who loves you dearly. — Anonymous

We readily confess our little faults in order to suggest that we have no big ones. — François de La Rochefoucauld

Do you know why the man who operates on people wears a mask? So if he really messes up, the patient won't know who did it. — Small boy to playmate

8

The Joy of Unmasking

Have you ever known an honest-to-goodness "mystery man," a Howard-Hughes-type character? I've encountered only one such person. He has become a legend in his own time. This fellow spends his vast riches in erratic ways, constantly travels throughout the world and, when least expected, pops up at a social event for a cameo appearance. Whenever he appears, he seems to look completely different. A human chameleon!

Talk about mystery, this fellow invented it. There are all sorts of wild tales about his antics. But most stories focus on his benevolence. Mr. X gives great amounts to needy causes. Perhaps this is why so many admire him, much as the early Californians admired Death Valley Scotty, who often threw bushels of dollar bills to crowds from the window of his private train.

It was a beautiful fall day when we boarded the plane for the Hawaiian Islands. My wife had managed to acquire another "deal" through her travel agency. We located our seats and buckled in. It was then that we noticed a slovenly-looking man in the front cabin area. Suddenly he grabbed the stewardess, took her to the row where we were seated, and demanded that a fragile-looking lady get out of his seat. (She had moved over after the door was closed, assuming the seat was vacant.) The embarrassed stewardess kindly requested that the bewildered lady move.

After taking his seat, the insistent man began making life miserable for everyone in the row, including us. He complained loudly whenever anyone needed to step by him, laughed uncontrollably at the movie, and intimidated the woman he had so discourteously ejected.

At first he looked familiar, but I quickly suppressed the thought. I hoped that I didn't recognize him. Then my unconscious mind produced an undeniable recall. It was the "mystery man," the same person considered by so many to be gracious and generous, the epitome of gentlemanly kindness.

In those five hours of flying, Mr. X went from being a candidate for sainthood to being my nominee for Mr. Obnoxious of the Decade! He never did recognize the two of us. Consequently, at social occasions where we've since seen him, he is once again disguised as Mr. Nice Guy. How can this man maintain two fiercely competing identities? His life must be extremely complex.

Masks Too Good to Lose

We've all encountered persons like Mr. X, people who display a respectable image around those they seek to impress, but the opposite with those they consider insignificant. Such individuals have mastered the devious art of mask wearing.

But *all* mask wearing is not bad. In fact, in some situations, mask wearing can be fun. Going to a party dressed like a clown or ghost is an example. We delight in assuming the role of another for a few hours, especially if everyone is costumed.

And what about seeing a favorite play where performers skillfully assume the identities of various characters? We do not berate the actors because they have set aside their true selves. Instead, their "legitimate hypocrisy" can be entertaining and admirable.[52]

Furthermore, our daily lives demand a certain amount of role-playing. In *As You Like It* (II. vii.), William Shakespeare declared:

> All the world's a stage,
> And all the men and women merely players:
> They have their exits and their entrances;
> And one man in his time plays many parts.

We must all do things we don't feel like doing—go to work with a headache, be friendly with those we dislike, or fix a flat tire in our best clothes. We force ourselves to carry out such distasteful assignments and rely upon God's Spirit within to keep us from becoming resentful.

Also, we must constantly change masks to adapt to different situations. We wouldn't dare speak to our boss as we do to our children. Nor would we act in church as we do at a ball game. As "civilized" persons, we know that we must constantly change our performances. Every situation has its own rules to which we must conform. Few people like rebels. Persons who insist on "making waves" are generally rejected.[53]

Social psychologist George Herbert Mead made a distinction between two parts of the "self": "I," the private, innermost person,

---

[52]Charles R. Swindoll relates an interesting connection between the mask and the generic term for "hypocrite" in the ancient Greek plays. "Did you know that the word 'hypocrite' comes from the ancient Greek plays? An actor would place a large, grinning mask in front of his face and quote his comedy lines as the audience would roar with laughter. He would then slip backstage and grab a frowning, sad, oversized mask and come back quoting tragic lines as the audience would moan and weep. Guess what he was called. A *hypocritos*, one who wears a mask." Charles R. Swindoll, *Improving Your Serve: The Art of Unselfish Living* (Waco: Word, 1981), p. 117.

[53]This fact was demonstrated in a social psychological experiment in which ten small groups of paid participants were gathered for problem-solving exercises. A "confederate" (a person in on the secret) was placed in each group, with instructions to mildly disagree with the consensus. Then all group members were asked to vote on one person who should be eliminated due to a shortage of funds. In all ten groups, the "winner" was the person who "made waves."

and "me," the role-playing, mask-wearing part of self that adapts to others' expectations. According to Mead, if we are to be well-adjusted adults, we will develop a healthy "me" as well as a robust "I." To "do our own thing" in spite of all can only spell catastrophe. Role-playing cannot be discarded or ignored.[54]

In summary, role-playing is vital to our well-being and can even bring enjoyment to our lives. It is essential, in spite of what many well-meaning Christian writers have said.[55] There is truly a sense in which we must be "in the flow" of society, in the world, although not of it.

Masks That Pinch Our Faces

Nevertheless, as we saw in the case of Mr. X, role-playing can get out of hand. It can damage us and harm those with whom we associate. Under what conditions does role-playing go sour?

When the "me" overtakes the "I" we're in trouble. We must always be more than our performance. There is a kernel self that must be continuously cultivated and protected. And that self must be balanced against the role-playing part of our personality. Scores of movie and sports stars have allowed their social images to smother their private selves. As a result, they sometimes rely on alcohol or drugs, or become suicidal.

Our masks must be consistent. To act too far out of character, even at a masquerade party, is distasteful and unwise. Recall that Mr. X became a completely different person when he perceived himself to be anonymous. Role-playing must be guided by consistent values and attitudes. To be compassionate, then harsh; jovial, then depressive; scrupulously fair, then radically dishonest cannot be tolerated within the role behavior of the

---

[54]See George Herbert Mead, *Mind, Self, and Society: From the Standpoint of a Social Behaviorist* (Chicago: University of Chicago Press, 1934). The same theme is presented in Erving Goffman, *The Presentation of Self in Everyday Life* (New York: Anchor, 1959).

[55]Christian writers often make the general statement: "We must get rid of all masks." The opening sentence in a book by Charles R. Swindoll is: "Okay, everybody, masks off!" *Dropping Your Guard: The Value of Open Relationships* (Waco: Word, 1983), p. 9. The beginning psychology or social psychology student knows that the complete and indiscriminate stripping of defense mechanisms is extremely dangerous. Mask peeling is a much more complicated undertaking than many Christian (or non-Christian) writers realize or admit.

same individual. Some variation is healthy, but extremes must be avoided.

Although role-playing for purposes of cooperation is often commendable, that which intends to deceive, hurt, or acquire undeserved gain is to be soundly rejected. Recall the resentment we've all felt after buying an overpriced, unreliable product because it was misrepresented by a convincing salesperson! Don't slip on a new mask in order to take advantage of another person. To do so cultivates cynicism throughout our society.

Finally, wearing masks in order to hide deep insecurities is unacceptable. To do so is to reject making improvement. Also, it means that we perceive ourselves as unworthy. Our inner being cries out to be revealed in order to be accepted. We must respond to that cry in spite of the risk.

In summary, masks that bury the inner self, masks that are radically inconsistent, masks that attempt to deceive, and masks that hide deeply ingrained insecurities must be rejected! They must be peeled off continuously, for they have a way of growing back. To keep them off our faces is to know the liberating feeling of being open, transparent, and having firsthand knowledge of sincerity and honesty. Few things can compare to that.

This feeling of openness is much like taking a bath, pulling up the shade to let the sunshine in, or breathing country air. Also, it's knowing what it really means to have a satisfying measure of Christian excellence. Such openness allows the love of God to flow freely from ourselves to others. The barriers are removed and the floodgates are opened. Pure love can now pour forth as God intended!

Most of us are aware of the danger of wearing the wrong kind of masks. On others they look grotesque. On ourselves we feel that our God-created identity is totally camouflaged, submerged in an ocean of deceit. Why do we persist in wearing such masks?

Why We Play Damaging Roles

Although none of us is exactly alike, we tend to gravitate toward the damaging kind of role-playing for the same reasons.

First, some of us follow the example of one (or both) of our parents. It seems to come naturally and increasingly so as we get older. For example, a person whose father was a hypocrite will usually tend to imitate him.[56] I cannot help but think of child evangelist Marjoe Gortner, whose con-artist father threatened to drown him in bath water unless he memorized his sermons to perfection. That he did, for I witnessed one of his "performances" as a child in the late 1940s. With this kind of parental guidance, it is little wonder that he told *Time*: "I can't think of a time that I ever believed in God." But that disbelief didn't stop him from preaching for profit, long after leaving his mercenary parents. He was drawn to his father's teaching and example.[57]

Second, we wear masks in order to avoid painful consequences. To "face the music," to "take your licks," to "bite the bullet" is not delightful. So we fake it. Attempting not to look stupid, we use long Latin words instead of short Anglo-Saxon ones. Trying to look different than the poor person we are, we buy a few name-brand items to fool the world. We especially grope for our masks when we know we're guilty and fear someone might lower the boom. I mused about the letter a university student sent to her parents:

Dear Mom and Dad:

I'm sorry to be so long in writing. Unfortunately all my stationary was destroyed the night our dorm was set fire by the demonstrators. I'm out of the hospital now, and the doctor says my eyesight should return—sooner or later. The wonderful boy, Bill, who rescued me from the fire kindly offered to share his little apartment with me until the dorm is rebuilt. He comes from a good family—so you won't be surprised when I tell you we are going to be married. In fact, since you always wanted a grandchild, you'll be glad to know that you'll be grandparents next month!

---

[56]Parental influence is great. The strongest correlation, for example, related to child-abuse is whether you were beaten by your own parents. There are two predominant reactions: reactance (i.e., acting the opposite of one's parents) and compliance (i.e., responding as one's parents would). The latter is far more likely than the former, especially as one becomes older.

[57]"Hollow Holiness," *Time*, 14 August 1972, p. 45.

P.S. Please disregard the above practice in English composition. There was no fire. I haven't been in the hospital. I'm not pregnant. And I don't have a steady boyfriend. But—I did get a "D" in French and an "F" in Chemistry, and I just wanted to be sure you received this news in the proper perspective.

We also wear the wrong kind of masks to benefit from the status of another person. When we believe ourselves to be unworthy, we often ride piggyback on the identity of another self, even if that person is a product of our imagination. When mentally ill individuals resort to this, we describe them as having multiple personalities or hallucinations.[58] When we do it in a less pronounced manner, it is simply known as playing the role. Usually it is closely related to such things as fads, trends, crazes, and modeling.[59]

The temptation to imitate another individual is powerful. Ministers find themselves copying the style of Chuck Swindoll or Lloyd Ogilvie. Appearance-conscious Americans mimic the dress and hair styles of John Travolta or Demi Moore. Then there's the recent exhibit of the Mona Lisa in Tokyo. Many Japanese girls had plastic surgery to become permanent, although inexact, replicas of the lady with the famous smile. There is no end to the variety of masks that people will enthusiastically wear in order to gain a little borrowed self-esteem.

Finally, some well-intentioned people wear masks in order to cushion others from the crushing impact of the harsh realities of life. Far from being malicious, such role-playing is intended to soften life's blows by casting a more positive light on another's painful situation, whether it be incurable cancer, loss of employment, or outright rejection of a dream.

Every author fears his archfoe, the rejection slip. Realizing that he must be told when he is turned down, he still doesn't relish hearing that he is incompetent. He wants to be told in a nice

---

[58]Kenneth Bianchi, the so-called Hillside Strangler, was diagnosed as having multiple personalities. As Kenneth, he was a soft-spoken, courteous gentleman. But as Steve, he was a merciless murderer and sex pervert.

[59]See Jon Johnston, *Will Evangelicalism Survive Its Own Popularity?* (Grand Rapids: Zondervan, 1980), chap. 6, pp. 103-22.

way. An aspiring author in China was sent a rejection note from his government:

> We have read your manuscript with boundless delight. But if we were to publish your paper, it would be impossible for us to publish work of lower standard. And as it is unthinkable that, in the next three thousand years, we shall see its equal, we are regretfully compelled to return your divine composition. We beg you a thousand times to overlook our short sight and timidity.

What a contrast to the sign I recently spotted in a grocery store:

> All Shoplifters Will Be Merrily
> Beaten to a Bloody Pulp!

Both of these are insincere. The messages are exaggerated. The former is an inflated evaluation. The latter relies on brutal frankness for the purpose of humor. As Christians, we must find a middle ground. We must be both candid and sensitive, honest and compassionate. This is no easy task.

In attempting to balance reality with others' feelings, I have often been tempted to soften the truth. And it has been easy for me to rationalize. After all, aren't the feelings of people more important than principles? An affirmative answer to this has left me feeling justified in donning masks that shade the truth.

Although this issue hasn't been totally resolved in my heart and mind, I'm beginning to see dangers related to even this kind of mask wearing. There is always the chance that people will discover the real facts and hold me accountable for not "coming clean." In addition, it seems as though I am tempted to continue faking it, even after realizing that the whole truth would no longer hurt the person(s) involved. To represent the facts is to risk losing face and destroying other person's confidence in me.

It is vital that we understand the kinds of masks that exist—both harmless and harmful. In addition, we must fully comprehend the underlying reasons we wear our disguises. To do so is to take a giant step toward God's kind of openness, the kind that benefits the excellent Christian!

Let's explore what God's Word says about altering one's identity.

A Clarion Call to Sincerity

Although the Bible refrains from using the modern-day terms *transparency, openness,* and *unblocked interfacing,* the message comes through that God does not tolerate fakes. His servants must declare with Job of old: "And my tongue will utter no deceit" (27:4b).

The Old Testament reveals how Adam and Eve blatantly sinned and then hid behind the mask of innocence. That was after they had hidden from God. Facing their Maker, and confronted with their sin, Adam blamed Eve, and Eve blamed the serpent. God saw through their masks and blamed them both, expelling them from the Garden of Eden (Gen. 3:8-17).

Joshua clearly saw through Achan's mask of honesty and discovered that he had stolen spoils of war and hidden them in his tent. His dishonesty had resulted in a costly defeat for Israel's army. Achan was put to death and his property was destroyed (Josh. 7:18-26).

Israel's first king, Saul, pretended that he had been obedient. God commanded that he kill the Amalekites, as well as destroy their property. But Saul spared their wicked king, Agag, and kept the best livestock for himself. Soon thereafter God's prophet, Samuel, informed Saul that God had rejected his kingship (1 Sam. 15:7-22).

New Testament writers emphatically condemn those who live a lie. Paul declared, "Provide things honest in the sight of all men" (Rom. 12:17b, KJV). "Let us walk honestly ..." (13:13a, KJV). "Provid[e] for honest things, not only in the sight of the Lord, but also in the sight of men" (2 Cor. 8:21, KJV). "Now I pray to God that ye ... should do that which is honest ..." (13:7, KJV). In another passage he writes, "I pray ... that ye may approve things that are excellent; that ye may be sincere ..." (Phil. 1:10, KJV). He further advises, "Whatsoever things are true, whatsoever things are honest ...; if there be any virtue [*arete,* excellence], ... think on these things" (4:8, KJV).

In a similar vein, the writer to the Hebrews states, "Pray for us: for we trust we have a good conscience, in all things willing to live honestly" (13:18, KJV). Finally, the apostle Peter admonishes Christians to have honest conversation among the Gentiles (1 Peter 2:12a).

But, as with the other attributes of Christian excellence, we must look to the incarnate One as our model. Was sincerity a theme of his life and teaching?

In a key messianic passage of Isaiah, the prophet predicted that our Lord would be characterized by total honesty. In his inspired vision he declared, "Nor was any deceit in his mouth" (53:9). Never was there a more accurate prediction. Our Lord never said anything he didn't believe, profess anything he didn't feel, nor lay claim to anything he didn't possess!

Centuries have passed since his resurrection, and many uncomplimentary statements have been made about our Savior. He has been called a visionary, a fanatic, and a dreamer. But amazingly few have labeled Jesus an intentional deceiver. As Charles Edward Jefferson declares, "There is something so pure and frank and noble about him that to doubt his sincerity would be like doubting the brightness of the sun."[60]

Because Jesus embodied sincerity, he could not hold back the claim that he was the Good Shepherd (John 10:11,14), the Door (10:7), the Bread of Life (6:35), and the Light of the World (8:12) — even though he knew it would cost him his life. But he had to say it, because it was (and is) the absolute truth!

Jesus' incorruptible honesty prompted an outpouring of candid words from his lips. To the Pharisees, who wore imbedded masks of self-righteousness, he declared, "You belong to your father, the devil ... a murderer from the beginning ... and the father of lies" (John 8:44). This is certainly not the language of the counterfeit humble, the timid, or the politically-minded. It is the language of God's only begotten Son.

And Jesus demanded his kind of honesty from his followers. For example, in a day when people hid behind all sorts of oaths, he commanded that his disciples refrain from all swearing.[61] His

---

[60]Charles Edward Jefferson, *The Character of Jesus* (New York: Grosset and Dunlap, 1908), p. 64.

[61]The religious leaders of Jesus' time categorized "oaths" as binding or non-binding. An oath containing the name of God was thought to be obligatory throughout life. But if another name was used, a person could break the oath. As

words are plain and direct: "Simply let your 'Yes' be 'Yes,' and your 'No,' 'No'; anything beyond this comes from the evil one" (Matt. 5:37).

This is the Man we want and need, for he is our refuge in the time of storm. When we are deceived and disappointed, we can find comfort in the One who says, "I am ... the truth" (John 14:6). When we are weary and confused, we can rest our souls upon One who is more faithful than the stars. His voice inspires assurance and dispels all uncertainty and doubt. He soothes and heals us by being genuine!

What he teaches about God we can receive. What he says about the soul we can believe. What he declares about sin and its penalty we can accept. What he proclaims about victorious life we can hold on to. What he instructs we can do, assured that it is the best course of action. What he warns against we can shun, knowing that it will lead to destruction.

That is why, as his followers, growing in his excellence, we feel increasingly secure and satisfied with our Lord. Our hearts become evermore at peace as they rest upon the One who is completely sincere.

Results We Can Expect

As we grow closer to the Master, and learn of him (Matt. 11:28-30), we begin possessing his kind of genuineness. What does that mean in practical, everyday terms?

We have a self-concept that becomes progressively healthier and more positive. We come to see ourselves through the loving eyes of the One who was crucified for us. And as this occurs, we loosen our death grip on our damaging masks. Rather, we unashamedly desire to reveal more of a self that we have come to increasingly respect.[62]

Jefferson states, "Jesus was disgusted by the reasoning of the bat-eyed pettifoggers." In this Scripture he implied if you want to stress something, simply say it again. If people still don't get the message, quietly repeat it. Jefferson states, "The world should be a place where all the evidence needed to prove something true is that a man asserts it. Today's courts of justice demand oaths because Satan has corrupted hearts and rendered ordinary speech unreliable." Ibid., pp. 59-60.

[62]See Jon Johnston, "Symptoms of a Lack of Self-Esteem," in *Building Self-Esteem*, ed. Gene Van Note (Kansas City, MO: Beacon Hill, 1983), pp. 14-21.

With inner confidence, we realize that our unmasking need not rely on being with a group of unmaskers who meet for that sole purpose. Some people become extremely dependent on a closed, intimate group that cultivates deep introspection and revelation. They share innermost secrets. Emotions are given free reign—even to the point of such things as the primal scream. After laying bare their souls, such participants (sometimes called "groupie-bums") become locked into an unhealthy dependence on the group.

Unlike this kind of emotional "unclothing," biblical unmasking is not restricted to a set time period with unmaskers. Nor does it advocate unmasking for the mere sake of it, leaving the human psyche unprotected and vulnerable to a rigid group dependency. Rather, our masks are taken off in order to put on Christ! As Paul so aptly states, "You have taken off your old self ... and have put on the new self, which is being renewed in knowledge in the image of its Creator ... Christ is all, and is in all" (Col. 3:9-11).

The Holy Spirit increasingly helps us to discern which masks are harmful. As we previously discussed, some disguises are harmless while others are crippling. Therefore, all mask shedding must involve a careful obedience to his guidance.

As J. Kenneth Grider declared, every Christian should maintain a core of privacy. We need not feel compelled to reveal everything about ourselves. For example, it can be damaging to constantly disclose details about our preconversion life of sin. With the psalmist we can take comfort that "as far as the east is from the west, so far has he removed our transgressions from us" (103:12). There's no need to dwell on our precleansed identity, nor to willfully shatter the confidence of others by continuous revelations about our sordid past.

On the other hand, the Holy Spirit will guide us to peel off masks that cultivate unspiritual phoniness and outright deceit.

Finally, that same Holy Spirit will progressively inform us as to who should receive our revelation, and when. Certain people can be devastated by our complete unmasking. Others, with Satan's help, can be counted on to use newfound information against us as they twist the facts in a degrading manner.

In most circumstances people need relationships to deepen before they can benefit from candid revelations. My wife knew a woman for a brief period. Suddenly this woman decided that she wanted to become an intimate friend—instantly. At their next meeting she turned to my startled wife and announced, "I want to be your friend, and we can never really be friends until you tell me everything about yourself! Do it now." I assure you, her request was not granted, and for good reason. Relationships require time. So should self-disclosure. But again, God has provided his Spirit to guide us into knowing if (and when) disclosures should be made. We can rely on that with certainty.

It's All in a Name

To call ourselves Christian is to say much about the kind of identity we claim (or it should). The term *Christian* implies "miniature Christ," being saturated with his presence and nature so that we come to perceive human existence and relate to all persons as he did. That means manifesting sincerity and genuineness. Failure to do this is to take his name in vain.

It was reported to Alexander the Great that one of his soldiers, who also happened to be named Alexander, needed to be soundly disciplined for bad behavior. The soldier was dispatched to the great conqueror's presence. He was asked to confess and hastily did. After hearing the shameful admissions, Alexander turned to his namesake and made one simple statement: "Soldier, either change your conduct or change your name!" The same admonition applies to those of us who bear the name of our Lord. May honesty characterize our lives!

People are not looking for a friendly church as much as they are looking for a friend. — Bill M. Sullivan

Relationships are built up, like a fine lacquer finish, with the layers of kindness. — Alan Loy McGinnis

You cannot sprinkle the perfume of happiness on someone else without spilling a few drops on yourself. — Leo Charles Johnston, Sr.

How many Californians are needed to change a light bulb? Five. One to do the work, and four to relate with him in the experience. — Anonymous

9

Webs of Love

It's tough to be left out, excluded, overlooked, or neglected. When it happens, it is often hard to forget.

I recall trying out for P.O.N.Y. League baseball as a boy. Someone had observed my playing skills at a sand-lot game and suggested that I go for the "big time."

I could visualize it all: home runs, cheering crowds, perhaps even a major league baseball contract in a few years. My parents would be so proud of their son—the same parents I was presently requesting to purchase all the paraphernalia needed to play: glove, uniform, shoes.

The coach of my team was a Christian. He was eager for me to do well, so that I might be a positive influence on the other fellows. That is why he gave me every chance possible. I was on the starting line-up in the first game.

Then my balloon popped. The dream vanished. I began what seemed like an endless string of strike-outs. Everyone tried to advise me, but things didn't improve. The poor coach continued to play me, to his chagrin. I did okay in practice—it was daytime. But under the glaring lights, before the boisterous crowd, my performance was pitiful. Finally, even my patient coach was forced to face reality. He had the team to consider. I had to be replaced immediately!

The skipper broke it to me gently, but I was intensely hurt. He asked me to sit in the dugout and watch my teammates play the game I loved. To cease being an enthusiastic, full participant. To become a mere pinch hitter, which really meant being an uninvolved spectator. The message was clear: I was no longer a part of the team. Banished to the bench!

It was painful to even look in the faces of the other players. They were well aware of my demotion and realized that I was no longer a participating member of their team. It wasn't long before I could take the rejection no more. I turned in my uniform—and with it my dreams.

But in retrospect, my situation wasn't nearly as bad as it seemed. My performance merited my exclusion. I had been given my chance. Also, I did have the option of quitting. Often in life, people must continue under the dark cloud of rejection. The apostle Paul was such a person.

No Welcome Mat

For well over a decade after his conversion, Paul was not fully accepted by his church. Shortly after being born again on the Damascus road,[63] and after being filled with the Holy Spirit

---

[63]J. Kenneth Grider offers references to substantiate that Saul (Paul) did receive his conversion on the Damascus Road. It is implied that he was entirely sanctified three days later with Ananias. Something revolutionary occurred when Saul saw the heavens light up, fell to the ground, and conversed with the risen Christ. He immediately ceased being the main persecutor of Christians (Acts 9:3-6). He was called as a "chosen" (*ekloges*, a Greek word having salvation overtones) instrument to preach the gospel. And he was so called on the Damascus road before seeing Ananias (Acts 9:15). Saul twice called Christ "Lord" (*Kurie*, Acts 9:5; 22:8), using the identical Greek word used by full-fledged Christian, Ananias (Acts 9:10). Ananias approached Saul and called him "brother" (Acts 9:17). In so doing, he told him, at the outset, that he considered him to already be a fellow

before Ananias, he began preaching in the synagogues of Damascus — "baffl[ing] the Jews ... by proving that Jesus is the Christ" (Acts 9:22). Then he went to Jerusalem, where the disciples "were all afraid of him, not believing that he really was a disciple" (v. 26).

The disciples finally agreed to take a wait-and-see attitude only after Barnabas testified that Paul had "preached fearlessly in the name of Jesus" (v. 27). Undaunted, the apostle left Jerusalem to blaze a missionary trail for his Lord — starting churches, writing letters of inspiration, proclaiming the Good News. He encountered all sorts of persecution: prison, flogging, shipwreck, hunger (see 2 Cor. 11:23b-30).

After three years Paul once again decided to become part of the "team." So off to Jerusalem he treked, "to get acquainted with Peter" (Gal. 1:18). Although he stayed with Peter for fifteen days, he "saw none of the other apostles — only James, the Lord's brother." Talk about getting the cold treatment! Paul undeservedly received it!

But there was no quitting for the apostle. Although Satan no doubt tempted him to become discouraged, he traveled again. Congregations were organized. People were gloriously converted from all walks of life. But he did encounter problems along the way: outright rejection and persecution from the Jews and biting suspicion from Jewish Christians who knew Paul only as "persecutor turned preacher." For all the latter knew, he might reverse himself and once again begin persecuting them.

It wasn't until fourteen years later (seventeen after his conversion) that the missionary from Tarsus returned to Jerusalem with Barnabas and Titus. They went to discuss the issue of Gentile circumcision with the church leaders. For the first time Paul received complete acceptance. He joyfully recorded, "James, Peter and John, those reputed to be pillars, gave me and

---

Christian believer. Their encounter did not involve "conversion language." Ananias specifically told Saul that Christ has sent him so that he (Saul) might "see again and be filled with the Holy Spirit" (Acts 9:17). In conclusion Grider adds, "Of numerous commentators checked, almost none of them, whatever their doctrinal stance, take the position that [this] conversion did not occur on the Damascus Road." *Entire Sanctification: The Distinctive Doctrine of Wesleyanism* (Kansas City, MO: Beacon Hill, 1980), pp. 46-48.

Barnabas the right hand of fellowship when they recognized the grace given to me" (Gal. 2:9).

But what took them so long? Why the seventeen-year probation period? How could the Jewish early church keep Paul at arms' length when he so desperately reached out for fellowship and acceptance? We can only wonder and ask rhetorical questions.

Like Paul, do we all have a driving need for acceptance, to be part of a "team," rather than just a pinch hitter? Absolutely.

Suffering from Marasmus?

We're all born with a compelling need to belong. Belong we must—if we are to survive.

During World War II, orphaned babies were placed in a large institution. The accommodations were pleasant: new furniture, brightly colored toys, delicious food. Nevertheless, the health of the children began to deteriorate rapidly. Although there were no signs of disease, they stopped eating and playing. They then grew weak and began dying.

United Nations doctors were flown in to investigate. Their prescription: For ten minutes each hour, all children were to be picked up, hugged, kissed, played with, talked to. The orders were obeyed and, within a short time, the strange epidemic disappeared. The little ones brightened. Their appetites returned. Their toys were once again played with. And when their ten minutes came, they enthusiastically reached out their little arms to be picked up by the approaching nurses.

The doctors identified their fatal lethargy as marasmus and described it as "a mysterious and gradual emaciation of the body which seems to strike when others don't take time to show enough love."[64]

The same principle holds true for the elderly. Social disengagement leads to loneliness and eventual death. Our senior

---

[64]It is a medical fact that if a newborn infant is isolated in a closet for the first weeks of his life, separated from communication and touch, he will suffer irreparable brain damage and even death. Frederick II of Prussia conducted such a grisly experiment, attempting to prove that newborns, if left unattended, will begin speaking Latin on their own. As we might expect, the babies (although provided food and water) perished.

citizens feel the effects of such isolation perhaps more than any other group in our society. No doubt that is why senility is so prevalent and why postretirement life averages only four years. The cry of most older people was voiced to me by my father, shortly after his retirement: "Son, you can criticize me, accuse me, borrow from me, make fun of me all you want—but just don't ever leave me alone."

But we all have an irrepressible need to interact with others. This truth has been said in so many ways. John Dunne states, "No man is an island unto himself." Baruch Spinoza declares, "Man is a social animal." Reuben Welch, in his book by that title, asserts, "We really do need each other."[65] Lloyd Ogilvie says God created us to be riverbeds rather than reservoirs. There must be a constant inflow and outflow of social contact in our lives.[66]

That's why we socialize, converse, give gifts, smile. That's why we join so many organizations, some of which seem humorous:

> *Let's Have Better Mottoes Association.* Its goal is to replace worn-out slogans with creative ones, e.g., "It's not whether you win or lose, but how you place the blame."

> *Committee to Award Miss Piggy the Oscar.* This group is dedicated to the proposition, in the organization's words, that "all pork bellies are not created equal."

> *Man Will Never Fly Society Internationale.* The society maintains that mankind was never meant to wing it. Its motto: "If man were meant to fly, God would have given him propellers!"[67]

And there is much to gain by being sociable. Psychologist James J. Lynch researched the lives of seven thousand persons, ages thirty to sixty-nine, for a period of nine years. His conclusion was that outgoing, sociable individuals live longer and

---

[65]Reuben Welch, *We Really Do Need Each Other* (Nashville: Impact, n.d.).

[66]The Reverend Lloyd Ogilvie is former pastor of the Hollywood (California) Presbyterian Church and currently Chaplain of the U.S. Senate. The idea was taken from a sermon he presented on one of his national telecasts.

[67]Steve Lawhead, "Absurd Associations," *Campus Life*, July-August 1982, pp. 36-38.

healthier lives than those who are shut off from others. The former are more resistant to heart and circulatory diseases, cancer, and strokes—and are even less inclined to suicide.[68]

People refer to this phenomenon in many ways: assimilation, systemics, linkage, social webbing, or fellowship. But it all comes down to one important idea: We're all born with an insatiable inner need for meaningful interaction with others. Our beings possess an overwhelming desire for social ties. For strong webs of love, woven between ourselves and others. This need begins on the first day of our lives. It continues until we breathe our last breath.

What is the significance of this fact for Christians desiring to deepen in biblical excellence?

Fellowship: Keynote in God's Word

The Bible spotlights the concept of fellowship, beginning with the creation account in Genesis. Most of us believe that God created Adam to have fellowship with him. Soon thereafter, Eve was created for Adam—and for the same reason. God said, "It is not good for the man to be alone" (2:18).

Then the "first family" of Eden's garden blatantly sinned. Their sin, like any sin, caused their fellowship with God to be broken. Feeling guilty and ashamed, they hid from the presence of the One whose holiness made them feel worse. Their hiding probably hurt our loving heavenly Father more than anything else they did or could have done.

From this story we glean an important truth: Excellent fellowship depends on excellent character. Our hearts must be right with God and purged of all uncleanness (see chap. 4) before we can lovingly relate with others. In his reference to our fellowship with other Christians, John states, "But if we walk in the light [i.e., become increasingly holy], as he [God] is in the light, we have [his kind of] fellowship with one another ..." (1 John 1:7).

What a joy it is to relate with those who manifest his purity and love. No wonder it refreshes and uplifts us to meet together with other believers. David declared, "I rejoiced with those who said to me, 'Let us go to the house of the Lord'" (Ps. 122:1).

---

[68]"Socio-Feedback," *Time*, 16 January 1978, n.p.

Aware of its importance, the writer of Hebrews instructs us to "not forsak[e] the assembling of ourselves together ..." (10:25, KJV). And Jesus promises, "... where two or three come together in my name, there am I with them" (Matt. 18:20). Paul also states, "God ... has called you into fellowship with his Son Jesus Christ our Lord" (1 Cor. 1:9). Implicit is the idea that Christian fellowship is possible only because of his work within us. Because we are of kindred mind and spirit, our meeting together is special. Something marvelous occurs. The air is electrified with his presence.

Why do we share the Good News of the gospel? John provides the answer: "We proclaim to you [non-Christians] what we have seen and heard, so that you also may have fellowship with us. And our fellowship is with the Father and with his Son, Jesus Christ" (1 John 1:3). In other words, come and join us. His blessings are too good to be enjoyed by a select few. There is an abundance of power, peace, and joy to go around for all who will come and all who will invite his excellent love into their lives.

As excellent Christians, our primary goal in life must be to attract and disciple outsiders into our nourishing fellowship. That is why we are servants, live a simplified lifestyle, and are filled with the Holy Spirit (see Acts 1:8). As God guides us in weaving a "love web" around their hearts, our own love becomes increasingly more excellent.

Giving spiritual birth to one of his creation, for whom his only Son died, transcends the joy of giving biological birth. Or it should. It is like saying to someone lost in sin: "Welcome to an eternity of joy. Meet the greatest people in the world, the *koinonia*—the fellowship of believers—who are filled with God's own Spirit!"

Unfortunately, drawing sinners into Christian fellowship frequently ranks low on our list of spiritual priorities. No wonder nearly four hundred evangelical Christians are required, each year, to bring one new "spiritual baby" into our fellowship! But why? What sidetracks us from fulfilling the biblical imperative?

Why Webs of Love Aren't Woven

First, we get tangled in our love webs. We fail to distinguish between the urgent (i.e., what clamors for immediate attention) and the necessary (i.e., what is best to do for the long run).

We have a knack for getting lost in trivia and busywork, things that need some attention, but are not critical to kingdom business. In so doing, we're a lot like the man who kept arranging deck furniture on the Titanic. He was so busy that he didn't bother to look down at the water and notice that the ship was sinking. Somehow, our priorities are not God's priorities.

All too often our best time and energy are consumed in maintenance activities, duties that focus on keeping the church doors open: landscaping, repairing, ushering, meeting on boards.

And how could I possibly forget? Singing in the choir. While many choirs provide music which augments the worship of God, more valuable spiritual energy is consumed in making music for ourselves than perhaps any other area. We've heard the expression *a church with a choir.* I know of one that can, more accurately, be described as a choir with a church. There is no calling program, ministry to shut-ins, street witnessing. But there is a choir filled with people who are convinced that they're fulfilling their total spiritual obligation by performing musically. The deck furniture must be arranged!

The point is this: Music is needed. Maintenance is required. However, it must (at least) be balanced with authentic mission. Granted, reaching out to strangers is always more difficult—because it is more threatening. Besides, it is less satisfying to the ego than performing before our own crowd. Nevertheless, we must force ourselves to re-establish our priorities according to biblical standards. We must crash through the barrier of doing maintenance, and become involved in authentic mission.

Second, we weave our webs selectively. We "web in" those who we feel will get us ahead. As for all others, we put them **down** ("You are below me on the social ladder"), put them **on** ("I'll never let you know the real me"), or put them **off** ("I'll keep you from having an authentic relationship with me").

What specific kinds of webbing do we prefer? There is elitism. We gravitate toward those we perceive to be important, persons who have influence in society, Y.A.V.I.S. people (i.e., young, active, verbal/vigorous, intelligent, sociable). We think that our association with people "up there" can improve our own social standing.

Then there is nepotism, or limiting attention to relatives. Primary attention is given to kin relationships. There are Little League games for the children, weekend outings at the family cabin, and plenty of family reunions. We say to ourselves that God desires us to be concerned with our families, which is true. But he doesn't intend for us to neglect others.

Finally, there is cronyism. Put simply, this refers to pouring time and energy into involvement with the gang, the buddies, the crowd we run with. This small network is made up of people with whom we closely associate and about whom we deeply care, that clique of persons who seems like family.

There is an overpowering temptation to gravitate to these three webs. Here we receive "strokes," feel secure, feel accepted and even flattered.

Unless we are biblically convicted and prayerfully cultivated, we do not involve ourselves with unpredictable, risky, low-status outsiders. Too much can go wrong with such associations. But we *must*. God commands it. He expects it, even though it may seem difficult and unpleasant.

But in setting out to weave webs of love, in connecting with others in caring, redemptive relationships, what should we keep in mind? Here are some suggestions that can assist us.

Proceeding with Confidence

To begin with, it is imperative that we increasingly think in terms of "we" rather than "me." This is possible only if we counter a persistent, natural tendency to focus on ourselves.

The phrase *one another* is repeated no fewer than fifty-eight times in God's Word. Our perspective of concern must give priority to those with whom we share within Christ's body. Paul spells this out in his letter to the Philippian church: "Do nothing out of selfish ambition or vain conceit, but in humility consider others better than yourself " (2:3). Becoming even more specific, the apostle instructs, "Each of you should look not only to your own interests, but also to the interests of others" (v. 4). What is the basis of your advice, Paul? He answers, "your attitude [will] be the same as that of Christ Jesus" (v. 5).

We must see ours as a corporate, not individual, identity. And if we do, we will "rejoice with those who rejoice [and] mourn with those who mourn" (Rom. 12:15). In short, we will "live in harmony with one another" (v. 16). We will cooperate more than compete. Our Christian fellowship will continuously grow better. Or, as Charles R. Swindoll says, our church will become increasingly like grapes and decreasingly like marbles:

> Every congregation ... can choose to be a bag of marbles, single units that don't affect each other except in collision. Or ... a bag of grapes. The juices begin to mingle, and there is no way to extricate yourselves if you tried. Each is part of all. Part of the fragrance ... [and] sometimes we 'grapes' really bleed and hurt."[69]

Second, we must prayerfully take the necessary measures to prevent conflicts from growing. At times the web of love wears thin and becomes frayed. It must be repaired immediately. If left unattended, small misunderstandings can quickly lead to conflict and alienation so that the entire body is adversely affected.

Jesus provides helpful advice: "Settle matters quickly with your adversary.... Do it while you are still with him on the way" (Matt. 5:25). Similarly, Paul states, "... do not let the sun go down while you are still angry, [for in so doing you] give the devil a foothold" (Eph. 4:26-27).

Every golfer knows that divots (pieces of sod skinned off the fairway) must be replaced immediately. Then they will take root and once again become part of the sod. But if they are allowed to dry out and wither in the sun, they cannot be replanted, and an ugly scar is left. The analogy is obvious. Relationships taken care of quickly have a much better chance of healing without scars.

The first two suggestions mainly relate to love webs within the Christian fellowship. What about people who aren't yet a part (they display an interest in the Christian life), but have not been

---

[69]Charles R. Swindoll, *Dropping Your Guard: The Value of Open Relationships* (Waco: Word, 1983), p. 178.

fully identified with the body? The final suggestion focuses on such persons.

As excellent Christians, we must give primary attention to those who have not been fully incorporated into the church fellowship. This is as difficult as it is necessary. Our lives become tightly interwoven with Christians we have known for some time.[70] As a result, we become oblivious to newcomers or marginally involved persons. Our ignoring them makes them feel even more estranged.

Something else contributes to the wearing of such blinders. Martin Marty refers to it as the bigotry-brotherhood paradox. In simple words it means the higher the morale of our group, the more likely it is that we will construct thick walls that exclude outsiders.[71] We feel so good about "us" that we become totally unconcerned about "them."

Realizing these harmful tendencies, we must be on our guard. We must consciously plan to interact meaningfully with outsiders. One church with two thousand members asks them to greet four persons they don't know before greeting one they do know. Another church has newcomers go out to dinner with members. Creative plans abound and are working. The specific plan is not as important as the fact that action is being taken and that outsiders are being welcomed and integrated into the church body.

Typically, we do far better at simply welcoming persons than at slowly, patiently incorporating them. Many are given the "red-carpet treatment" as a first-time visitor to a church. We pin a

---

[70]Church-growth experts have stated that it takes an average of two years for a new Christian to become fully incorporated/assimilated into a church. In so doing, he separates himself from the "old crowd" (see 2 Cor. 5:17). Howard Snyder is quoted as saying that the church must constantly win new people to Christ. These persons still have linkage with the "world" and are able to relate to other people who are not Christians. To have a preponderance of second-, third-, and fourth-generation Christians is to risk having broken contact with the unconverted.

[71]Marty's term is elsewhere described thusly: "As we emphasize in-group unity, brotherhood, and oneness, we increasingly reject those unlike our kind. As a result our walls are built taller and thicker, our righteousness is increasingly paraded, and this causes an even greater rejection by outsiders." Jon Johnston, *Will Evangelicalism Survive Its Own Popularity?* (Grand Rapids: Zondervan, 1980), p. 71.

flower on their lapel and introduce them to the congregation. But then comes the letdown as people gravitate back to the cliques and ignore the outsider. We must realize that the welcome is only the beginning. As Paul declared, we must "become all things ... so that by all possible means [we] might save some ... for the sake of the gospel" (1 Cor. 9:22-23).

First, persons must be incorporated socially until they feel a sense of belonging and social comfort. This process follows a definite ten-step process (see Figure 2). Second, the same individuals must be assimilated psychologically until there is a mutual trust between themselves and the church members. This can be thought of as taking place in eight steps (see Figure 2). We must not be contented or rest until all persons in the body become fully incorporated and assimilated into the fellowship. To settle for less is to satisfy ourselves with something less than a New Testament church.

Well Worth the Effort

At least once a year our church has an open house and a special service for the parents of our day-school children. It is a relaxed, fun evening for everyone as we see the little ones perform in an uninhibited manner.

The teacher of our adult Sunday-school class foresaw an opportunity for us to become acquainted with our visitors. He made a strong appeal for all church members to be present and to be outgoing and friendly to the parents. So the church arranged to have light refreshments after the service.

Well, the time came for "us" to intermingle with "them." Unfortunately, few even bothered to show up. And those who did grouped together in a circle, totally excluding those for whom we had met.

It was frustrating, as you can imagine. Although the few of us who came managed to speak to all the visitors, we had little time to interact meaningfully, except with one couple who remained for a longer period of time.

These people were pleasant but thoroughly lonely, having just moved to California from the east. They complimented the church for its day-care facilities and began asking about the church. We invited them to attend. They immediately responded.

The next Sunday they were there, along with several other families we had managed to invite.

Figure 2 **Incorporation/Assimilation Scale***

Incorporation (Social)	-10	Knows nothing of a particular church
	-9	Aware of church but knows no one in the church
	-8	Knows someone in the church
	-7	Has a personal friend in the church
	-6	Has two or more friends in the church
	-5	Has been involved in a social event related to the church
	-4	Has visited the church
	-3	Is involved in a church activity (i.e., a Bible study, a recreational group)
	-2	Attends church frequently
	-1	Familiar with setting and worship style
	0	Feels sense of belonging and social comfort
Assimilation (Psychological)	+1	Conversion
	+2	Regular attendance
	+3	Baptism
	+4	Developing friendships
	+5	Church membership
	+6	Sanctification
	+7	Accepts responsibility
	+8	Trusted by membership

* From Win Arn and Charles Arn, *The Master's Plan for Making Disciples*, ed. Bill M. Sullivan (Kansas City, MO: Nazarene Publishing House, 1984), p. 44. Used by permission of James F. Engel.

The new couple began attending our Sunday-school class faithfully. Then following a progression they became involved in discussing the lesson, made friends with the other couples, accepted Christ as their Savior, and were elected officers for the class. The gentleman became the class president, a position he held for several years.

Our hearts were gladdened to see the couple attend every Sunday morning, both Sunday school and the morning worship service. However, few in the latter setting bothered to become acquainted with the "outsiders." It became embarrassing to need to reintroduce them to the members for months and even years. Even so, the new couple kept coming. Gradually they became more involved: teaching Sunday school, supervising the nursery, and serving on the church board.

Now they are fully incorporated and assimilated into our fellowship. The small efforts we exerted on the day-school open house paid rich dividends. Two beautiful persons were born into the kingdom of God and grew in Christian maturity. The church has accepted them in its web of love. May this scene be repeated scores of times in our congregation, as well as throughout all of Christendom!

Stand for something or you'll fall for anything. — Art Linkletter

What lies behind us and what lies before us are tiny matters compared to what lies within us. — Walt Emerson

When once I had seen the truth, there was no drug that I could take to make me unsee it. — Euripides

But, Dad, I gotta be a nonconformist. How else can I be like the other kids! — Teenager to father

10

Refusing to Cry "Uncle"

Do you remember B.D.A.C. (before the days of air conditioning)? I do. On a sweltering mid-August afternoon, we would open a window or eat an ice-cold popsicle. If the setting were Sunday church, we would fan ourselves. The local funeral home always provided an ample supply of fans, the kind made of cardboard. On one side was a picture of Jesus or a country church and on the other was an advertisement, such as, "Williams Funeral Home: The place with the convenient lay-away plan."

The point is this: We did survive, in spite of the odds. We literally didn't know what we were missing.

Today everything is different. Having the air conditioner malfunction is tantamount to having a three-alarm fire. It is a bona fide emergency. Next to food and water, it is a basic need for survival!

Why the change? It's simple. Our bodies have adapted to a new set of requirements. What once seemed uncomfortable seems torturous today. No longer does it seem "right" to endure high temperatures, even while eating ice cream.

In the same manner in which we adapt physically, we adapt morally to changing circumstances. Because of strong cultural influences, what once seemed right seems wrong and vice versa. We're swept along by the stream of social conformity, and the current is swift.

The key question is: Does God change as we change? Are his standards continuously adjusted to our own mindset and actions so that rightness and goodness are based on our unique situation?[72] Not at all.

We serve a God described by the writer of Hebrews as "the same yesterday and today and forever" (13:8). Our consistent God demands consistent obedience to his timeless commandments that he has recorded in his ageless Word. If there is adapting to be done, we must return to his changeless truths. He need not, as many seem to believe, adjust to the compromising pathways we have chosen.

As Christians who are deepening in biblical excellence, we will accept this important truth and live our lives accordingly. Furthermore, we'll be alert to the fact that we can be easily deceived by the perverted influences of our own culture. For, as Proverbs 16:25 warns, "There is a way that seems right to a man, but in the end it leads to death."

This means that we must have convictions and hold to them. Our convictions are our roots that connect us with the Source. Without them, we are little more than what Elton Trueblood terms "cutflower" Christians—shallow, frail, short-lived.

Mercedes-Benz ran an advertisement which stated, "Excellence begins with how high you set your standards." The same is true with Christian excellence. We must internalize and live according to God's lofty standards—but with his faithful guidance and strength. Then our growth in him is assured. Our spiritual roots tap into his inexhaustible supply.

---

[72]Situation ethics, a philosophical and religious viewpoint articulated by Joseph Fletcher, maintains an absence of objective standards. According to this belief, each situation demands its own response in accordance with the ethic of love. So, for example, if you subjectively deem it "loving" to commit adultery with your neighbor's wife, that is the best course of action.

Notice that I said "live according to his standards." Many, like the Pharisees of old, rigidly maintain convictions that are not ordained by him. As Fritz Ridenour once said, "They are so straight they make an arrow seem like a snake." But it does them no good. In fact, it brings them great harm, pushing them in the opposite direction of his kind of excellence. What are some examples of such convictions?

Standards That Stifle

First, some convictions are little more than superstitions. They are based on a notion, emotion, quirk, or illusion.

Such fuzzy thinking is to be expected among pagans. In 600 B.C. the ancient Greeks were being defeated in battle. A philosopher advised that the Areopagas be covered with statues of all known gods. Then a flock of black and white goats was allowed to roam on the same hill while the Athenians carefully observed. Whenever a goat lingered in front of a particular statue, the name of that god was written down and he was later worshipped. Stories involving the use of such superstitious reasoning can be compounded. Without knowledge of God's truth, such foolish measures are frequently taken.

But as Christians, we should know better. We need not rely on oracles, wizardry, shamanism, or blind fate. Our God is personal and reasonable. There is nothing mysterious about his commands, and they are as near to us as his Word.

In his famous tract, "Plain Account of Christian Perfection," John Wesley offered seven warnings to sanctified Christians. The second one was: "Beware of ... enthusiasm." In that day, "enthusiasm" meant what he termed "heated imagination." We know it as fanaticism. The father of Methodism went on to say that dreams, voices, impressions, visions, and revelations are not good sources for determining our standards. He declared, "They may be from God. They may be from nature. Or they may be, and often are, from the devil." It is far better to receive guidance from his voice in prayer and by reading his written Word.

Second, some convictions attract attention for a selfish ego. When our appearance, speech, or behavior is eccentric, we stand out in the crowd. We separate ourselves from the masses. In short, the focus is on us. The reaction can be felt embarrassment or often pride.

In his great chapter about love, Paul declares, "If I give all I possess to the poor and surrender my body to the flames, but have not love, I gain nothing" (1 Cor. 13:3). What could attract more attention than these "noble" acts of sacrifice? But even they, if motivated by selfishness rather than *agape* love, are to no avail.

We must have convictions and stand by them consistently, regardless of the reactions of others. We owe no explanation, for we have received our direction from the Maker of the universe. However, we must not maintain and manifest such convictions in order to showcase a self that is eager to be in the spotlight.

Third, some convictions are generated by an unwillingness to accept change. People deny the new by hiding behind traditional beliefs and conduct.

A few centuries ago the church rejected scientific advancement. Galileo, Copernicus, and de Perthes were branded heretics for suggesting alternative conclusions. Inventions were denounced. For example, Sir James Simpson declared chloroform to be "a decoy of Satan that blesses women [during childbirth], but in the end hardens them and robs God of the deep, earnest cries that should arise to him in time of trouble."

Today some of us also slide into a "conviction rut" in order to avoid facing change. We become closed to such things as alternative ways of disciplining our children, different ways of communicating with our neighbors, and contrasting methods of serving our God. We're in a rut, which one person defined as "a grave with both ends kicked out." We have our security and don't wish to alter our set course.

To accept such a mind-set is to thwart our growth and to bring about an inevitable, traumatic collision with reality. We must not allow our standards to be used as vehicles of escape.

Finally, some convictions are exclusively negative. These convictions are perceived as sheer duty that we regard with distaste, do with reluctance, and later resent.

Augustine declared that the goal of all religion should be to enjoy God, not to chafe under the cloud of a rigid, negative ritualism. Why? If we are rigidly ritualistic, we picture God as a stern taskmaster rather than a Being of infinite love and excellence.[73]

Our convictions must liberate rather than imprison. They should resemble the tightness of a violin string, which provides the musician with the ability to use that string for maximum melodic potential.

Certainly we must avoid self-defeating and God-dishonoring convictions. But the biggest problem does not lie in possessing the wrong variety of convictions nor even in having corrupt motives that underlie such standards. Rather, it is a severe erosion of any convictions.

The Drift Toward the Precipice

A small animal was seen riding on a log just above Niagara Falls. While swimming in the still water he had no doubt climbed onto the floating piece of wood to rest. Soon it began to move, at first slowly and then more rapidly toward the falls. He had a choice. He could either quickly jump off and swim back or he could continue with his joy ride. He chose the latter. According to eyewitnesses, he reached the churning rapids just above the falls. It was too late to jump. He clutched the log. As he saw the tremendous drop approaching, his fur stood up and his eyes bulged. Some shrieks of terror were heard. Then there was silence as he tumbled through the air to his doom.

Many of us compromise our convictions in a similar manner. We begin with good intentions. Rather than being malicious, we're simply careless. Our fateful course typically follows these steps:

1. Refrain from compromise but forget why. The reasons for our convictions fade, and we become confused or less certain.
2. Begin going against our convictions and feel guilty.

---

[73]Dean Kelley differentiates between *stricture* and *stringency*. The former is "systematically imposed by leadership." Such enforced norms lead to low morale. On the other hand, *stringency* occurs "spontaneously among the adherents." In contrast to stricture, stringency yields high morale. Dean M. Kelley, *Why Conservative Churches Are Growing: A Study in Sociology of Religion* (New York: Harper and Row, 1972), pp. 109-11.

3. Continue compromising until we feel less and less guilty.
4. Become oblivious to the convictions we once held so dear.[74]

In my own childhood, Sunday used to be a day of rest. After church we'd read good books (or be read to), sleep, engage in quiet conversation, sing around the piano. Sunday buying was totally unacceptable. We reasoned: Store clerks should rest too. It is God's day.

Then I "jumped on my log" to begin my drift toward compromise. As an "I'm-ready-to-begin-thinking-for-myself" teenager, I began to assert my independence. The plan was clever. I would pay the store clerks on Saturday for everything I'd be coming to get on Sunday. Then I could get around the Sunday-buying standard while technically not getting into trouble with my conscientious parents who reluctantly went along with this practice. I boasted about my ingenious scheme to everyone. By using brainpower, I had managed to sidestep the "oppressive" Sunday-is-a-day-of-rest routine. But, what is more significant, the drift had begun.

Today, Sunday buying is commonplace for me. It began with restricting purchases to "essentials." But now, everything desired is considered essential. And I don't even feel guilty. I should.

We all have a strong temptation to climb onto the logs of compromise. The drift begins. We justify ourselves by claiming that we're being liberated. We're breaking out of the constraining fetters of legalism. Standards held in a previous time, when we were less enlightened, were foolish. In fact, we get a little embarrassed when we even think about them.

Granted, we must mature as the times change. What is considered worldliness in one era is not in another. As we grow in grace, God does help us to be more discerning. We know all that. But the temptation to drift is always present—especially with second-, third-, and fourth-generation Christians who have

---

[74]The "worldly squeeze" is a gradual but directional process. Sociologists of religion think of it as occurring in three stages: (1) *accommodation*, toleration of cultural/societal values (legitimization); (2) *assimilation*, cooperation with cultural/societal values (participation); and (3) *amalgamation*, fusion with cultural/societal values (identification). Jon Johnston, *Will Evangelicalism Survive Its Own Popularity?* (Grand Rapids: Zondervan: 1980), p. 36.

received their convictions secondhand. And, for some strange reason, all drifting that I know of is in the direction of becoming more liberal. What was previously considered wrong is now considered right—instead of the other way around. This fact concerns me greatly!

What does God's Word have to say about our convictions? Let's explore.

The Bible's Perspectives about Convictions

God's Word addresses the subject of this chapter directly. We know that the excellent Christian is commanded to obey, and to obey completely. As Samuel told disobedient King Saul, "To obey is better than sacrifice ..." (1 Sam. 15:22). What are we to obey? The commandments that are contained in the Bible.

What does obedience to his Word have to do with biblical excellence? Everything. Jesus tells us that our obedience is God's measuring stick for determining how much we really love him. You will recall that love and godly excellence are the same. John's Gospel recorded these words of our Master: "If you obey my commands, you will remain in my love, just as I have obeyed my Father's commands and remain in his love" (15:10). That is plain enough. God's directives to us must be obeyed. In fudging on them, we only wreak havoc for ourselves.

Biblical instruction approaches the subject of convictions from two perspectives: one negative and the other positive. One is focused on avoidance and the other is directed toward the dividend of such avoidance. But it should be remembered that they are opposite sides of the same coin.

We are told to reject the subtle temptation to become worldly. John 15:19 tells us that we "do not belong to the world." Romans 12:2 instructs us to "not conform any longer to the pattern of this world." James 1:27 warns us "to keep [ourselves] from being polluted by the world." Then, in 4:4 he declares, "Friendship with the world is hatred toward God." Perhaps the strongest verse of all is 1 John 2:15: "Do not love the world or anything in the world. If anyone loves the world, the love of the Father is not in him."[75]

In simple language, what does it mean to be worldly? It is to be world-like—to think, feel, believe, act, and live like those whose lives are not under the lordship of Christ. It is an attitude of the heart.

Fritz Ridenour presents a helpful analogy. In his graphic words: "The old cliché compares Christians with ships and the secular world with water. The idea is that ships are to sail through the water, but water isn't supposed to get into the ships ....[God] is on the bridge shouting, 'Man the pumps!'"

But there is another side to this coin. Our motivation to consistently hold onto our convictions must be based on more than fear of disobedience. We must maintain our principles in order to enter into the abundant life that he has provided for us (see John 10:10) so that we might possess a full measure of his grace and reach our God-given potential.

What does it mean to live the abundant life? Revelation 3:15-16 tells us that we will keep our spirits and commitment at the boiling point. A lukewarm, halfhearted response to Jesus will vanish. Paul, in his Second Letter to the Corinthians, promises that our heavenly Father will "always [cause] us to triumph in Christ" (2:14a, KJV). He adds, "Through us [he] spreads everywhere the fragrance of the knowledge of him. For we are to God the aroma of Christ among those who are being saved and those who are perishing" (2:14b-15).

Is there anything else? The apostle also promises that "God richly provides us with everything for our enjoyment" (1 Tim. 6:17).

All of this and enjoyment too! What more could the world hope to offer?

Realizing the overwhelming dividends of obedience to God, we see our convictions and standards in a positive light. Rather than constraints, they are liberators. Rather than spirit-dampers, they are the very springboards that vault us to genuine fun and enjoyment. It is with good reason that author Jess Moody

---

[75]L. A. King, "Where 'the World' Hangs Out," *Eternity*. November 1981, pp. 25-27.

declares, "Fun was one of the chief characteristics of the apostolic church. 'Hilarious' was a New Testament adjective used to describe the saints."[76]

It is little wonder that Christians growing in excellence cease thinking in terms of what commandments they can sidestep. Instead, their line of reasoning is exactly the opposite. They ask, What more can I do, say, and be to reflect godliness and the abundant life? They do not seek to prove anything or earn God's favor. Rather, with cups overflowing, they yearn to nestle closer to the One they love most and to reflect his purity and power to the lost world.

In contrast to those motivated to compromise, Christians deepening in love "drift" in the direction of tightening up, getting rid of excess worldly baggage, even going a little overboard in sacrifice, as Mary did when Jesus came to visit. You'll recall that she poured perfume, her love gift, over her Lord's feet (John 12:3). It was pure nard, and one full pint, costing a year's wages. She definitely went overboard. But so did her Savior—for her, for all of us!

We draw strength and direction from God's Word on this critical issue. Convictions count with him. We must have the right kind, and stick by them come what may. But he promises to guide.

What practical suggestions might be offered to those of us who desire to develop a principled life?

Unbending Knees

Like Shadrach, Meshach, Abednego, and Daniel, who refused to bow down before King Nebuchadnezzar's golden image in ancient Babylon, we must keep stiff knees before the gods of compromise in our day (see Dan. 3). God expects us to stand tall in purity and expectancy. In resolving to not bow, the following suggestions could prove to be helpful.

First, we must be certain that our security is in God rather than in the reactions of men. Paul tells us to "serve wholeheart-edly, as if [we] were serving the Lord, not men, because [we]

---

[76]Jess Moody, *A Drink at Joel's Place* (Waco: Word, 1967), p. 19.

know that the Lord will reward everyone for whatever good he does ..." (Eph. 6:7).

As pilgrims in a foreign land, we can expect adverse reactions from those serving the spirit of the world. We cut across the grain of their basic nature. We rub them the wrong way.

Success, in the eyes of this world, means conforming to its pattern. This pattern Watchman Nee describes as the "mind behind the system," in short, the satanic principle which governs our planet (see Eph. 2:2).[77]

But when we strive for God's kind of excellence, an attainable standard rather than an elusive goal like success, he calls the shots. We have a heavenly Quarterback. What he tells us we do, knowing that his way will lead us to eternal victory — no matter how heated the "game of life" becomes.

The point is simple: We cannot please the world and God at the same time. In his high-priestly prayer to the Father, Jesus said that his disciples were hated by the world. Why? "For they are not of the world any more than I am of the world" (John 17:14).[78]

To overlook this important fact and to try to straddle the fence between God and Satan — in order to receive this world's acclaim — is a losing proposition. Short-term suffering might be avoided, but in a matter of time, the disguise must be lifted. And both God and men charge betrayal.

As our Lord said, "No one can serve two masters" (Matt. 6:24). When we try, we can only gravitate toward the master of this world — Satan. But by choosing one Master, our heavenly Father, and considering his approval more than sufficient, life becomes fulfilling.

Second, we must be extremely careful in deciding what convictions to embrace. When we prayerfully and sincerely study the Scriptures — as did Paul's church at Berea (see Acts 17:11) — God's Spirit will guide us "into all truth" (John 16:13). Once his truth is lodged in our hearts and minds, we are able to

---

[77]Watchman Nee, *Love Not the World* (Wheaton: Tyndale House, 1968), p. 38.

[78]"The child of God will be involved in conflict with evil powers, and with Satan himself, if he earnestly undertakes to possess all that God has promised to him on this earth" (cf. Ephesians 1:3, 6:10-18). "Introduction to Joshua" in *Oxford NIV Scofield Study Bible* (New York: Oxford University Press, 1984), p. 225.

determine which things in our lives are in opposition to that truth.

What are such things? The mother of John Wesley sent a letter to her son, who was a student at Oxford University. It contained a stated rule of thumb concerning what kinds of convictions to have. Her words were wise: "Whatever weakens your reason, impairs the tenderness of your conscience, obscures your sense of God, or takes off the relish of spiritual things, whatever increases the authority of your body over your mind, that thing for you is sin."[79]

May we likewise avoid all such things that dull the keen edge of our Christian experience and testimony. For to so indulge is, of certainty, to be willfully disobedient to the One who loves us so.

Finally, we must always remember that while biblical principles are general, convictions are personal. Convictions flesh out God's eternal principles in our individual lives so that his will is adapted to our unique situations and circumstances. This implies that we all have a tailor-made mission to fulfill with God's continuous direction.

Weaker Christians are known to have one strong tendency: being much harder on others than themselves. They castigate, condemn, judge. Psychologists term this projection, the practice of seeing our own weaknesses in others and criticizing the same harshly.

Christians growing in excellence become increasingly less judgmental of others and harder on themselves. They understand why Jesus sounded such a definite warning against all judging. The Master declared, "Do not judge, or you too will be judged" (Matt. 7:1). Just how are we judged by judging? Jesus continued, "For in the same way you judge others, you will be judged [by God], and with the measure you use, it will be measured to you" (v. 2). As our standards for others go up, God's expectation of us rises. That's plenty of incentive to put all measuring sticks away at once.

---

[79]A. F. Harper, "Wisdom and Appetite," *The Enduring Word Adult Teacher: Great Topics of Wisdom Literature* (Kansas City, MO: Nazarene, 1984), pp. 34, 36.

Nevertheless, we must bear down on our own commitment. As Canon H. P. Liddon once said, I must have a "heart of iron to myself [i.e., demanding], a heart of flesh to my neighbor [i.e., accepting], and a heart of fire [i.e., commitment] to my God."[80] By making certain that we are being true to the convictions he has given us, we become the best possible witness to the unsaved.

Jesus was such a model, and he attracted so many during his sojourn on earth. That's why those people found themselves spontaneously asking him, "What must I do to be saved?" He told them, and they were.

Some Are Persecuted

Convictions—the kind that really set us apart from others—can make us feel more than a little uncomfortable. If we're not careful, we can begin feeling sorry for ourselves. Whenever I am tempted to do that, I remember those whose faith cost them dearly.

My wife and I accompanied a group of university students to an oppressive country where few smile. All colors seemed drab. Freedoms that we take for granted were absent.

One of our students was granted permission to visit with an uncle. His visit lasted several hours. Upon his return, I couldn't help noticing that he was visibly shaken. In fact, he was crying as he told of what his relative had conveyed.

A Christian, the student asked the members of his uncle's family whether they were Christians. They responded by telling of the kind of persecution all believers endured: loss of opportunity to attend college; loss of membership in the official Youth Corps, which meant loss of job; continuous surveillance and harassment that included removing telephones and censoring mail. The list continued.

Then came the naive question: "But what if you would live a secret Christian life? What if your faith in Christ would go undetected?" His uncle explained that the government had ways of detecting true Christians. For one thing, Youth Corp meetings were scheduled during church times and attendance was com-

---

[80]Canon H. P. Liddon, quoted in an editorial by William McCumber, *Herald of Holiness*, 1 September 1982, p. 16.

pulsory. He continued, "And even if you stay away from church—or refrain from verbally sharing your faith—they would still know if you're a true Christian." How? "It is obvious to them that you are living a different kind of life from that of others."

With such cold, calculated oppression, are there those who live the Christian life? Many. And the numbers are growing. As "brands plucked from the burning," there are the courageous ones refusing to cry "uncle" to Satan and defying the threatening ultimatums of their government.

Just a few thoughts about their plight were enough to motivate me to hold fast to my convictions. Their steadfastness strengthened my own. May it strengthen yours.

We cannot without God, but God will not without us. — Anonymous

Die when I may, I want it said of me that I plucked a weed and planted a flower wherever I thought a flower would grow. — Abraham Lincoln

The greatest asset is to have a liability; the greatest liability is to have no liability. — Louis Mann

The world is filled with willing people: Some willing to work, and the rest willing to let them. — Robert Frost

11

We Are All Gifted

It's an oft-repeated adage: Spiritual gifts — use them or lose them. My wife and I have attempted to use our talents in the work of God's Kingdom, but separately until last Christmas.

Our church asked us to be co-narrators for the beautiful cantata "He Started the Whole World Singing." We were elated, for it was an opportunity to perform at our favorite church before our favorite people. Best of all, we'd be doing it together, using our God-given vocal talents.

We rushed out to purchase matching outfits. Then the rehearsals began. They were arduous, but necessary for the kind of perfection we planned to attain. Before long, the music and narration flowed together. This was bound to be an experience long remembered!

The big night arrived. Every seat was filled early. The decorations were immaculate. As anticipation soared, the choir filed in. My wife and I took our places behind the microphones. The dramatic prelude began. Everything went without a hitch. There was a standing ovation which seemed to never end. Did we ever feel fulfilled *together*!

The people demanded an encore performance a week later. They wanted to hear the concert again and to invite their friends to share in the experience. How could we turn them down?

My wife checked our calendar and noticed that some good friends from Illinois would be visiting on the day of our repeat performance. They had never been in our home or our church before. It was perfect timing. We would treat them to the evening of their lives. After all, we should narrate even better the second time.

Preparation once again took place. Clothes were readied. Lines were rehearsed. Then our company arrived, and we sat down to dinner. It wasn't long before the conversation drifted toward our church and the upcoming event. Our guests were overjoyed to know that they would be seeing us perform. In addition to the Rose Bowl game, this would be a highlight of their trip.

Then the telephone rang. The voice on the other end was abrupt. The response was one of shock. "We have what?! ... Been replaced? Oh, replaced." No reason was given. Our lines had simply been given to someone else. And what an uncomfortable time we had breaking the news to our bewildered friends. They just looked at us. Then we all started laughing. Before long, everything was in perspective again. We concluded that it was another of life's curve balls. And we had struck out swinging.

We've all had high hopes of serving in an important capacity, only to be told, "Sorry, we've had a change of plans. You won't be needed after all." Intense disappointment followed, along with the temptation to refuse when asked again. Some of us have muttered to ourselves, "If this is the way people are treated, no wonder they hesitate to become involved. Few enjoy being a masochist!"

The truth is that many of us do resist using our God-given spiritual gifts for his glory. In biblical parlance, we put our "candle ... under a bushel" (Matt. 5:15, KJV). Often this is not our preference. As we observe the overworked, overexposed minority do everything, we find ourselves wishing that we could have a part, for God's kingdom and for ourselves. Why are our aspirations short-circuited? Let's examine some possible reasons.

Roadblocks and Detour Signs

The first two reasons focus on why some of us have never started to utilize our natural endowments in service to God. They can be perceived as roadblocks.

First, many of us feel inferior. As a result, we develop an intense shyness and timidity. We think, "When you're as bad as I am, you don't take risks. Instead, I must hide. Not behind trees, like I did when I was a child, but behind excuses and in the shadows of those who are more qualified."

Those of us who are multitalented have less temptation to withdraw into passivity. When one gift fails, another can be pulled out of the bag. There's always a support system. But when we possess only one talent—the minimum allotment for every human being created by God—there is a tendency for us to bury it.

Jesus supports this conclusion in his parable of the talents. The person given five talents went at once and gained five more, as did the one with two talents. "But the man who had received the one talent went off, dug a whole in the ground and hid his …" (Matt. 25:18). The ones with hefty endowments increased them and flaunted their gain. But the poor fellow who was given one gift hid it. He did not just hide it, but he buried it in the ground. The thought of having to explain his poor stewardship later no doubt made him want to climb into the same hole!

The world expresses this principle graphically. "When you're hot, you're hot." "It takes money to make money." "When you've got it, flaunt it." This implies, "When you're not hot, you're cold." "When you don't have money, forget trying to make it." "When you don't have it, don't look to get it."

Many sociologists believe that the overpowering temptation for the single-gifted person to hide it is intensified in a large church. It is easy to be anonymous. Also, it seems foolish to compete against superior talent. The conception (or misconception) is: With this many people, there must be enough talented people to fill all areas of responsibility. Ministers of large churches would argue with this conclusion, but it is a pervasive belief nevertheless and has some justification.[81]

A second reason why we fail to employ our God-given gifts is that we allow time to sneak up on us. We are convinced of the importance of using our talents for God. We're not timid. We intend to get involved—some day. But we procrastinate. And, as one writer put it, "Procrastination is the thief of time."

All of life can legitimately be perceived as a race against the clock. Someone described middle age as "that period of life when we try to use up what Mother Nature has given us, before Father Time takes it away."

Unfortunately, we often fail to comprehend the brevity of life. James describes man as "a mist that appears for a little while and then vanishes" (James 4:14b). But regardless of our illusions, earthly existence is finite. There is an end as well as a beginning. The average man lives but seventy-four years.[82] That is approximately 888 months, 3,848 weeks, 27,010 days, 648,240 hours, 38,894,400 minutes and 2,022,508,800 heartbeats. One writer focuses on life's brief stages:

> Tender teens,
> Teachable twenties,
>   Tireless thirties,
>   Fiery forties,
>   Forceful fifties,
>   Scared sixties,

---

[81]A complete treatise about the small church in relationship to super church is presented in *The Smaller Church in a Super Church Era*, ed. Jon Johnston and Bill M. Sullivan (Kansas City, MO: Beacon Hill, 1983). Special mention of the participation factor in the small church is on pp. 31-32, as well as in other locations.

[82]Average life expectancy (A.L.E.) has varied throughout human history. For the ancient Romans it was thirty-eight years. For Native Americans today, it is forty-four years. It should be noted that the variance is mostly due to infant mortality. For example, in Ecuador, 60 percent of all children die before age five. That, of course, lowers the overall A.L.E. When Americans point with pride to the fact that the A.L.E. for males is seventy-four years, it must be remembered that this figure differs little from the one mentioned in Psalm 90:10: "The length of our days is seventy years—or eighty, if we have the strength; yet their span is but trouble and sorrow, for they quickly pass, and we fly away." In short, the A.L.E. has varied little in the course of history. People unencumbered by disease or war seem to live a life that averages the "threescore years and ten" (KJV) that is mentioned by the psalmist.

> Sinking seventies,
> Aching eighties,
>   Shortening breath,
>   Death,
>   The sod,
>   And God.

My college roommate, Mike, had a sign on his desk. I thought about it often, and even memorized the words:

But one life,
t'will soon be past.
Only what's done for Christ
will last.

In my world travels, I have observed the ruins of man's greatest achievements: the Jerusalem temple, the Egyptian pyramids, the Temple of Diana in Ephesus, the Great Wall of China. All that remains are crumbling, flaking rocks. But the words of Mike's poem penetrated my mind most deeply when, last summer, I visited Caesarea in Israel. It was King Herod's crowning glory—the same Herod who killed Bethlehem's male babies, trying to murder baby Jesus.

The year was 12 B.C. The haughty king invited the world to Caesarea for the Olympic Games. People came from everywhere to the golden city of enchantment. The featured event was horse racing, held in the city's extravagant Hippodrome.

After providing this historical background, our guide stopped the bus beside a huge cornfield with banked sides. Some Arab farmers toiled in the hot sun. Beside the road was a columned arch. It was all that remained of Herod's famous Hippodrome, once the envy of the ancient world. Today, it is only a tourist site.

Only what's done for Christ will last.

Life is short. There is no time to waste. Yet we do, and with the best of intentions. Like the rich man in God's Word, we keep building our own barns and saying to ourselves, "You have plenty of good things laid up for many years. Take life easy; eat, drink and be merry" (see Luke 12:16-21). "There is no need to become involved in God's work today. There's always tomorrow," we say to ourselves.

But these are roadblocks that keep people from ever getting involved. What about those of us who are attempting to use our God-given talents for his work—as my wife and I did when volunteering for the Christmas Cantata? What are some detours that throw us off track, send us in the wrong direction, or put us on a road where we can only spin our wheels?

First, it is quite possible to be replaced, even when we feel deeply that we are fulfilled and in the center of God's will.

Sometimes we're forced to bow out, or at least to take a position of less recognized importance. Someone thought to be more talented comes along. No longer is our advice or participation requested. We're shelved.

Second, often we fall prey to overexposure and over-involvement. We try to do too much, for ego sake or because others refuse to pick up the torch of responsibility.

As a result, we feel taken for granted by the apathetic and overlooked by those who bestow credit. Oh, we keep trying, but what we once did joyfully becomes burdensome. Rather than anticipating, we dread. An acute case of burnout sets in. We go through the motions, without a real sense of mission.

In the secular world, this is a day of specialization. A Gallup Poll listed the multitude of job titles held by Americans. To read some is to smile. Can you imagine having these listed on your job resume: Teabag Stringer, Tombstone Polisher, or Chicken Sexer (the person who examines the underside of baby chicks to determine whether they are male or female). During summers of her college years, my wife held such illustrious employment positions as Pitter (removing seeds from peaches) and Huller (separating almond shells from the outer hulls). Truly, this is a day of specialization. The advantage is that one person doesn't have to be an expert in all areas. That means a lot when everything is so complicated and seems to be getting more so.

It is unfortunate that what we have learned in the marketplace we often fail to apply to the church. God made us all specialists by granting us specific spiritual gifts. To attempt to do everything, including what others should (and could) be doing is to eliminate the possibility of reaching our God-intended potential. Our heavenly Father does not want us to drive ourselves to burnout, which can only render us useless. We must avoid this detour at all costs!

What wise instruction does God's holy Word give us about the use of our spiritual gifts?

Using Our Loaves and Fishes

It was time for the Passover feast. But the crowds, on their way to Jerusalem, were intent on seeing and hearing the Man who was performing miracles. Five thousand of them followed him to the hillside overlooking the Sea of Galilee. As he spoke they were mesmerized. They lost track of time.

Jesus became concerned about their need for bodily nourishment and shared that concern with some of the disciples. Philip threw up his hands in frustration: "Eight months' wages would not buy enough bread for each one to have a bite!" (John 6:7). But Andrew located a small boy with five small barley loaves and two small fish. After revealing this to the Lord, he sadly declared, "But how far will they go among so many?" (v. 9).

Christ saw an opportunity for a miracle as well as an important spiritual object lesson. After he said grace, the food was multiplied. All five thousand were well fed and twelve "doggie bags" full of leftovers were collected. What was the lesson? The One who said, "Anyone who will not receive the kingdom of God like a little child will never enter it" (Mark 10:15), chose to use the gift of a powerless lad. The bearer of the gift was lowly, without power and status. He was simply an intrigued youthful bystander. In addition, the gift that he bore was insignificant in the eyes of the world. His loaves were probably mashed and stale. And we all know what happens to fish that has been exposed to the hot sun.

The only component of value in this entire scenario was the boy's willingness to present his gift to the Master. He offered all he had. That is what God wants of us. As John D. Rockefeller said at the dedication of the United Nations Building in New York City, "We are stewards of all God gives us—and that for a little while." To begin with, it is necessary for us to lay our loaves and fishes at his feet—willingly, and even cheerfully. As Paul states, "Not reluctantly or under compulsion, for God loves a cheerful giver" (2 Cor. 9:7). But in presenting our gifts to the Master, what does God's Word instruct us to keep in mind?

First, we all have a special and unique sphere of influence. There are people only we can reach. Somehow we have earned their attention and trust. They listen to what we say, and do what we do. As a result, in the biblical perspective, they are our responsibilities.

Jesus talks about the "faithful and wise servant" the master puts in charge of the other servants while he is on a trip (Matt. 24:45-51). Such a person is in charge of the household. In effect, Jesus is saying that we are all in charge of something. We all have a "household." The Greek term for "household," *oikonomia*, literally means "sphere of influence." We must accept our responsibility with the utmost seriousness. Our best gifts and talents must be conscientiously appropriated to the task at hand, for we are our Master's representative, operating under his authority and power. There must be no holding back, no laziness, no "passing the buck." The One who enables us to effectively serve — who generously provides us with spiritual gifts — expects us to fulfill our mission.

Second, the sharp distinction we have made between "minister" and "layman" must be revised according to biblical direction. We are all ministers within our circles of influence, be they on the job, at school, or at church.

James L. Garlow's *Partners in Ministry* contains some rather startling statements: "Religion is too serious a business to be left to the clergy." Also: "If football is twenty-two men on the field who desperately need rest, and 60,000 in the stands who desperately need exercise," church can be described as "a few desperately weary clergy — being cheered on by many spectators who desperately need the essential exercise of ministry."

Garlow points out that the New Testament word for "layman" (*laos*) means "person of God." That's not something to be taken lightly. Peter, in his first epistle, lists five things every "person of God" is: a living stone (resting on the cornerstone, which is Jesus); a chosen person; a royal priest; a citizen of a holy nation; and one of God's very own persons (2:4-5, 9-10). In short, we are authentic ministers of the gospel![83]

Where does this leave our professional clergy? Are they still needed? Absolutely. Freed from having to motivate us to minister, they can become equippers, teaching and training us to be "work[men] who [are not] ashamed and who correctly handle the word of truth" (2 Tim. 2:15). In addition, they can become "player-coaches" who take the lead in being as well as doing. Paul instructs Timothy: "Set an example for the believers in speech, in life, in love, in faith and in purity" (1 Tim. 4:12). In short, they are master shepherds who head a church of under-shepherds in caring for God's sheep.

Finally, after recognizing our sphere(s) of influence and considering ourselves authentic ministers, we must begin to prayerfully minister in accordance with our spiritual gifts.

Some of us aren't sure which gifts we possess. To begin with, we should consult the lists of gifts in God's Word. Kenneth Kinghorn has summarized them (see Table 1).

---

[83]James L. Garlow, *Partners in Ministry: Laity and Pastors Working Together* (Kansas City, MO: Beacon Hill, 1981), pp. 11-22, 39.

Table 1[84]

Romans 12:6-8	1 Corinthians 12:4-11	1 Corinthians 12:28	Ephesians 4:11
Prophecy Teaching Serving Exhortation Giving Giving Aid Compassion	Prophecy	Prophecy Teaching	Prophecy Teaching
	Healing Working Miracles Tongues and Their Interpretation Wisdom Knowledge Faith Discernment	Healing Working Miracles Tongues and Their Interpretation	
		Apostleship Helps Administration	Apostleship
			Evangelism Shepherding

After becoming aware of the potential gifts, we must attempt to pinpoint our strong and weak areas.

Refer to the Trenton Spiritual Gifts Analysis in Appendix A. This simple test can be of great assistance in determining those areas that we should be most intent on cultivating. Grade the test and read the specific scriptural references that apply to your highest scores (i.e., your strongest gifts). Spend some time in prayer of intense commitment and for guidance as you proceed to develop and use your spiritual gifts. This exercise can be extremely rewarding.

---

[84]From *Gifts of the Spirit* by Kenneth Kinghorn. Copyright © 1976 by Abingdon Press. Used by permission.

A Needed Perspective

First, with God's help, we must chart a steady course as we use our spiritual gifts for him. This means directing our primary attention to our heavenly Father. He bestowed our talents in the first place. He helps us refine and effectively utilize those talents in his kingdom. He deserves all praise when others respond favorably to our display of spiritual gifts.

When we accept that everything is in his hands, we can rest patiently (i.e., be in a state of expectant readiness; see Ps. 37:7). When that occurs, life ceases to be in discord. Instead, there is harmony and rhythm, meaning and fulfillment. We are neither demolished by insult nor unduly inflated by compliment. We know we're dependent upon him.

Knowing this fact had a positive effect on Paul, who was persecuted. Acts 28:15b declares, "Paul thanked God and was encouraged." Like one concert violinist who kept his eyes riveted on his teacher in the balcony, so the apostle fixed his eyes on his Master (see Heb. 12:2). Paul's life became like a beautiful symphony. His course was steady. He was at peace.

Second, in being a faithful steward of our spiritual gifts, we must be more concerned with internal fulfillment than external applause. To receive his smile is to be rewarded. Or, as 2 Timothy 2:15 puts it, being "approved of God" is the ultimate.

Like secular excellence (see chap. 2), Christian excellence focuses on a standard rather than a goal. However, you will recall that Christian excellence is a self-imposed measurement based on personal potential, whereas secular excellence is what this world deems important and rewards with the only currency it possesses: power, privilege, and wealth. But as Christians, our standard is God's unchanging Word. In addition, it is to increasingly reach our potential for using our spiritual gifts for his glory. Unlike the world, our divine Paymaster rewards our growth process as well as our final product.

For us, it matters not who looks or who looks the other way. We do not depend on their fickle reactions for our satisfaction. Nor do we envy those who succeed. As the psalmist says, we do "not fret when men succeed in their ways" (34:7b). Success that is derived from Christian excellence, received in gratitude and reconsecrated to God is entirely commendable. Success outside this realm is not enviable because it is its only payment.

People are not our master. Nor are the trinkets they wave before our eyes as they attempt to lure us in their direction. Rather, we serve One who penetrates deeper than the external. He rewards the deepest recesses of our inner spirits with an indescribable joy.

This kind of joy Carl Lewis gave witness to before the international media. He unequivocally stated that his greatest satisfaction in life is his vibrant, personal relationship with Jesus. Standing beside this, his record-setting four gold medals pale in significance! He, like all of us who have embarked on the journey of Christian excellence, can anticipate that ultimate reward on the day of judgment when our Lord will address us by name and say, "Well done, thou good and faithful servant: thou hast been faithful over a few things, I will make thee ruler over many things: enter thou into the joy of thy LORD" (Matt. 25:21, KJV).

Finally, as our spiritual gifts yield ever-increasing dividends, we must increase in generosity. As my father used to tell his parishioners, "We must give until it hurts, then give some more—until it quits hurting." As was emphasized in our Lord's reaction to the widow's mite (Luke 21:1-4), all giving to God must be sacrificial. He deserves, and desires, the best that we have.

It was a snowy Sunday morning, the day before a soldier was to go to war. He attended the morning worship service at his church. The offering plate was passed. Later, while counting the money, the ushers noticed a crumpled note. Scratched out in pencil were two simple words: One life. Rather than tossing in a few coins, the soldier had offered God all that he possessed.

We are asked to do the same. What does our divine Master require of us? Everything. Recall the story of the servant left in charge of his landlord's household (Matt. 24:45-51). The steward neither had nor made any claim to ownership. His task, like ours, was to conscientiously apply the best of his abilities to the responsibilities he had agreed to assume—undergirded by his master's complete blessing and authority.

As God increases our responsibility and prosperity, we must do more than say thanks and hoard his gifts. Our task is not barn-building or fortune-amassing. Rather, we must forever realize that we are given more in order to give more. Our tight fists must relax as we allow its contents to slip through our fingers and land on areas of severe need. These areas are close to the heart of God.

This Takes the Cake!

Stewardship is the business of all of us. We are all gifted by our loving Creator. Each gift given us, no matter how seemingly insignificant, is capable of being infinitely expanded. When gifts are expanded and appropriated, God is glorified!

My recently deceased mother-in-law was reared in a Kansas farm community as an orphan. She was always shy, choosing to stand behind people at a social gathering. Her feelings of inferiority were many and intense. She would cover her mouth when smiling, not allowing others to observe her facial expressions.

Although she was a committed Christian, she'd be the first to admit that she was not richly endowed with spiritual gifts. In fact, it took many years for her to discover one. But that one discovery made all the difference in the world—even though it isn't listed (except by inference) on the official biblical list of gifts.

It began when, just for fun, she entered a local baking contest. To her amazement her entry, a chocolate layer cake, captured the first-place ribbon. It was the first honor like this that she had ever received. Immediately she was invited to enter the winning recipe in the Butte County (California) Fair. Again she won. The recipe was featured in the *Best Cooks of the West: Butte County Cookbook*. All of her friends, and scores throughout the city, read about her winning entry. She became known as "that great cook" (a well-deserved title, to which I can personally attest).

Mom began to take great comfort in what she perceived to be her one and only talent. It gave her some confidence in other areas of her life—but areas always related to baking. Then she began to use her spiritual gift for the Lord. She started a baking ministry. She made cookies, cakes, and pies for convalescent homes throughout the town. That kept her busy, but extremely fulfilled.

God blessed her unique service to his kingdom. Before long, the recipients of her benevolence began telephoning. They shared their joys as well as their heartbreaks. And she listened. Others began attending her church—and kept attending.

Without a doubt, Mom's gift, when returned to God in humble obedience, was multiplied in its effects. She left us with a helpful, encouraging lesson: We're all truly gifted, even those of us who, by comparison with others, possess fewer of God's bestowments. As the song declares with certainty: "Little is much when God is in it!"

There are three things which cannot come back: the spent arrow, the spoken word, and the lost opportunity. — William Barclay

Any direction, just so it be forward. — Anonymous military general

The journey of a thousand miles begins with one step. — Chinese proverb

No problem is so awesome, so complicated, so fraught with danger that the average citizen can't run away from it. — Charlie Brown (*Peanuts* comic strip)

12

Daring to Act

During my years in seminary I knew him as a prolific scholar, captivating professor, intense ping-pong competitor, and absent-minded friend. This man was so absent-minded that the favorite student pastime was trading accounts of his unbelievable antics: mailing his wife's groceries, or walking home after forgetting that he had driven his car to town.

His life was a study in contrast. From a humble, even primitive, childhood home in the Ozarks, he ascended to (and excelled in) educational institutions of renown. He once wrote an autobiographical article, which he appropriately entitled "From the Ozarks to Oxford."

Perhaps the simple and impoverished roots caused his deep compassion for the needy. He spoke of that concern often. So did his colleagues. It was the trendy thing to do in the late 1960s.

But there was a difference when *he* spoke. A certain pathos in his voice betrayed a firsthand experience. The pain of destitution had been indelibly etched on his psyche. As a result, he manifested the depth of empathy that only direct involvement can provide.

His kind of empathy made him discontent with secondhand information. He yearned to once again feel the gnawing pangs of hunger, the extreme discomforts of crowded living conditions, to learn more about the plight of the have-nots, and even to identify with them in their misery. So he decided to act.

My compassionate professor put on ragged clothes, grew a shaggy beard, and set out for the ravaged, restless inner cities of America, not for a few token days, but for many long months. He limited himself to the jungle-like survival tactics of his desperate neighbors: begging for meager handouts, sleeping in the rat-infested doorways of slum apartments, and competing for degrading jobs, only to repeatedly endure cold rejection.

Finally, it was time to return to that "sophisticated jungle" we know as civilized, middle-class America. But he returned with renewed and expanded insight that was generously shared with, and deeply affected, students like myself. We received a wealth of valuable, firsthand information and along with it, an inescapable burden for the forgotten, powerless, and destitute of our land.

But even more impressive than the captivating experiences he shared and the subsequent knowledge we gleaned was his courage to act, to depart from his understanding family and follow his compelling heart to the scene of his great concern — the ghettos of our nation.

Like him, we must dare to act. To put ourselves on the line To have enough courage to break the fetters of apathy and respond to our heartfelt convictions.

Our actions need not be as radical as his. God guides each of us to follow our own star. But the inescapable fact is that we all must act. We must assert ourselves in faith. Withdrawal can lead only to loss of function, as any of us who have had a broken arm in a cast can attest.

This is not to minimize excellence of mind and intention. But, as we read in chapter 4, we must move on to excellence in loving deeds. In so doing we learn firsthand that our heavenly Father guides, empowers, and rewards those who lovingly assert themselves in his name.

Give Me This Mountain!

Most of us can recall from childhood Sunday-school lessons the story of the twelve Hebrew spies who scouted the land of Canaan (Num. 13-14). Although ten of them saw conquest as impossible, Caleb and Joshua said, in effect, "Let's go for it. With God by our side, we will conquer!" Their plea fell on deaf ears. Fear gripped the people and they even "talked about stoning" (14:10) these advocates of virtual suicide. Moses was influential enough to prevent that. But the Hebrews refused to act. Instead, they wandered aimlessly in the Sinai Desert for forty years.

By then Moses had died. Joshua had assumed leadership of the nation as God directed. The belated command was given, and God's people invaded Canaan. They conquered the cities, one by one. But all the nation was not purged of Canaanites. Stubborn pockets of guerrilla fighters remained, especially in the treacherous hill country.

Who would step forward with the necessary leadership skills and courage to drive them out? Caleb, the son of Jephunneh! Unlike the much younger spy of forty, he was now a white-haired senior of eighty-five.

I can imagine the scene. Everyone's favorite grandfather enters the tent of his commander-in-chief, Joshua. Joshua says, "Good afternoon, Caleb, how are you feeling today? Is your rheumatism acting up again? Are you remembering to take your medicine? It's necessary, you know."

With a spark in his eye, the elderly gentleman replies, "Forget about my aches and pains, Joshua, I have something to tell you. And I want you to listen carefully."

> I was forty years old when Moses ... sent me from Kadesh Barnea to explore the land. And I brought him back a report according to my convictions, but my brothers who went up with me made the hearts of the people melt with fear. I, however, followed the LORD my God wholeheartedly. So on that day Moses swore to me, "The land on which your feet have walked will be your inheritance and that of

your children forever, because you have followed the LORD my God wholeheartedly.

Now then, just as the LORD promised, he has kept me alive for forty-five years since the time he said this to Moses, while Israel moved about in the desert. So here I am today, eighty-five years old! I am still as strong today as the day Moses sent me out; I'm just as vigorous to go out to battle now as I was then. Now give me this hill country ["Give me this mountain," KJV] that the LORD promised me that day. You yourself heard then that the Anakites were there and their cities were large and fortified, but, the Lord helping me, I will drive them out just as he said. [Josh. 14:7-12]

Caleb was saying, "I'm ready for action. It's time to take care of business. Let's go with God!"

If I had been Joshua, I might have put my arm around the old fellow and said, "Caleb, your spirit is commendable. Your attitude is a fine example. You certainly haven't lost your fight. But we must be reasonable. You're twenty years past retirement. Why not relax now? Go find a comfortable rocking chair, and hold your grandchildren on your lap. Let the rest of us take it from here on."

But Caleb was a person of action, old age or no old age. Joshua must have known this, for he granted his request. The area of (and surrounding) Hebron was given to Caleb to conquer (v. 13). Conquer he did—which is not unlike most persons of action.

The pertinent question is: Why do many of us who are younger and more able-bodied than Caleb hesitate to accept a soul-stretching challenge? Why are we, as Fritz Ridenour puts it, "about as swift as a speeding glacier" when it comes to pushing ahead to action? Let's examine some reasons.

Why Deeds Are Short-Circuited

There are almost as many reasons for nonaction as there are persons who avoid taking action. But perhaps the most conspicuous of these reasons should be explored.

First, many of us would rather talk than act. We've heard the expression "talk is cheap," and it is. Our verbiage can provide us with a convenient illusion of involvement.

We do a lot of talking on a university campus. Great quantities of information are imparted, discussed, and responded to on examinations. But there is little action. This fact prompted one of my colleagues to declare, "I often feel that my teaching is like filling a bathtub with facts. At test time, the student pulls the plug and all goes down the drain at once. And there's not even a 'ring of memory' left." In addition, students aren't given sufficient opportunity to act upon what they do retain.[85]

For many of us, talk is easy and action is hard. And because of this, inactivity reigns. We're affected by what the late author and missionary to India, E. Stanley Jones, termed "the paralysis of analysis."

Second, some of us possess a nonassertive temperament. Whether it's because we were born that way, or became that way through conditioning, we find it more "natural" to avoid taking action.

It is important that we understand our basic temperament and pinpoint our strengths. As the Seven Sages advised, "Know thyself." A Greek physician, Hippocrates, outlined four temperament types which have been consistently referred to through the centuries. They are sanguine (happy, chatty, forgetful); choleric (leaders, drivers, dominating); melancholic (thinkers, perfectionists, sensitive); and phlegmatic (calm, easy-going, indecisive).

Refer to Appendix B, which provides a more thorough explanation of the types and a simple test for determining one's temperament type.

---

[85]I have recently noticed some significant movement in academia to provide students with opportunities for action. For example, in-class experiments as well as out-of-class fieldwork illustrate abstract principles. My own university has instituted a tutorial program for juvenile offenders at Camp David Gonzales. The wards are taught math, English, and related courses on a one-to-one basis. Our students report that such action on their part yields increased self-confidence, more sensitivity to human need, greater understanding of the outside world, and expanded ability to conceptualize the connection between theory and reality.

Third, some of us avoid action because we realize that it involves risk. To act is to take a chance of something going wrong:

> To laugh is to risk appearing the fool.
> To weep is to risk appearing sentimental.
> To reach out for another is to risk involvement.
> To expose feelings is to risk exposing your true self.
> To place your ... dreams before the crowd is to risk loss.
> To love is to risk not being loved in return.
> To live is to risk dying.
> To hope is to risk despair.
> To try is to risk failure.[86]

The faint of heart and the unwilling of spirit hesitate to take such risks. For them it is good enough to remain tucked away in the secure nest of inaction.

Fourth, some of us refrain from doing because we think that others will (or should). Someone jokingly defined a college president as a person "who looks at the dirtiest, meanest job and tells his assistant to get it done at once." Passing the buck is easy to do, especially when we know that there are others who can or will take action. In social psychology, this principle is known as the bystander effect.[87]

Action-oriented persons are likely to assume responsibility, regardless of who might (or should) be involved. Completing tasks is primary in their estimation.

Finally, more than a few of us sense an inner need to be passive and await our destiny. We believe in fate. What's "written in the stars" is believed to be certain and inescapable.

---

[86]Seen in *Humanican*, an informal newsletter for Youth Agency Administration students at Pepperdine University, 28 January 1982, p. 2.

[87]John M. Darley and Bibb Latane have studied the conditions under which people become willing to help one another. Their interest in the subject was generated by the Kitty Genovese story. She was murdered, although for one-half hour she screamed and cried for help while thirty-eight persons witnessed the event. No move was made to help her or even to call the police. The researchers found statistical support for the following principle: *The more people that are present in an emergency, the less likely it is that any one of them will make a helpful action.* Lawrence S. Wrightsman, *Social Psychology in the Seventies* (Monterey, CA: Brooks/Cole, 1972), p. 34.

Such a belief destroys ambition, and "can do" optimism is evaporated. The only thing left is to receive what fate has in store and to adjust accordingly. I heard an amusing story about a fatalist who tumbled down a flight of stairs. He got up, brushed himself off, and with a big smile said, "Well, I'm sure glad that's over." In other words, it was bound to happen; I just didn't know when. Now that the suspense is over, I can relax until the next blow of fate.

Without a doubt, this (or any) kind of fatalism can kill enthusiasm for action. What's the use? If all is predetermined, what difference can our efforts possibly make?

There are other defeating short-circuits to action: becoming sidetracked by trivial matters, expecting reward for everything done, or awaiting the right kind of leadership. The list is seemingly unending.

What does God's Word say about the necessity of taking action? Are there specific directives that we must seriously consider? Let's explore.

The Christian Action Manual

The Bible can rightly be perceived as an inspired account of how God has acted on our behalf in history. He acted not because we earned or deserved it (see Eph. 2:8-9), but because of his unconditional, limitless, and excellent love.

When our hearts become saturated with the same love, we too will act. We will make a committed effort to spread his love through deeds and actions. We do this not to earn his favor (see Titus 3:5), but as an outgrowth and natural response of our love for him. What does God's Word declare concerning action taking in the life of the Christian?

First, we are commanded to pray for godly action to take place. Without such action, God's kingdom will not expand on earth.

Curtis Mitchell has written an intriguing article which strongly suggests that our Lord never prayed directly for the eternal salvation of lost souls. In addition, Paul offered but one explicit prayer for the latter (Rom. 10:1). Certainly both cared deeply for the unsaved.[88] How, then, did they choose to pray?

Instead of praying for the harvest, our Lord chose to entreat God for the harvesters, the ones who would take action under the Father's power. In Matthew 9:37-38 we read: "Then he said to his disciples, 'The harvest is plentiful but the workers are few. Ask the Lord of the harvest, therefore, to send out workers into his harvest field.'"

Similarly, when Paul was imprisoned he penned a letter that requested prayer not for his release from prison, but rather for his effectiveness in preaching the gospel. Ephesians 6:19-20a declares, "Pray also for me, that whenever I open my mouth, words may be given me so that I will fearlessly make known the mystery of the gospel, for which I am an ambassador in chains" (see also Col. 4:3). He requested that the believers pray for him as he proclaimed the message of salvation.

Why didn't he request prayer for his fellow prisoners, mentioning them by name? He knew that their condition would be miraculously improved if only he could share with them in the power of God's Spirit. It was for that power that he prayed.

In short, our prayers are to be directed toward effectiveness in witnessing: the opportunity to witness (Col. 4:3), the courage to witness (Eph. 6:19), the message of witness (Eph. 6:19). We must focus our prayers on having God's blessing and help as we act in his name.

Second, the Bible instructs us to actively seize opportunities whenever they arise. We are to respond to God-sent chances to reveal God's love rather than allowing them to slip through our fingers, never to be recaptured.

John Greenleaf Whittier spoke the truth when he declared, "For of all sad words of tongue or pen, the saddest are these: 'It

---

[88]In several instances, Christ and Paul prayed for the unsaved indirectly. Jesus instructed us to "pray for those who persecute you" (Matt. 5:44, NASB). The greatest benefit for such an unsaved persecutor would be his conversion. Similarly, Paul argued that prayers be offered "for kings and all those in authority, that we may live peaceful and quiet lives in all godliness and holiness" (1 Tim. 2:2). Behind his immediate objective is a more crucial one, that God "wants all men to be saved and to come to a knowledge of the truth" (2:4). Thus, prayer for unsaved government officials is implied. Curtis Mitchell, "Don't Pray for the Unsaved!" *Christianity Today*, 16 September 1983, p. 28.

might have been!'" To realize that we didn't but might have taken action can make us feel regret, especially when another's eternal destiny is at stake.

In the Book of Romans, Paul offers timely advice for the growing Christian (12:9-13). One of his instructions is: "Seize your opportunities" (v. 11b).[89] Another source offers the alternative rendering: "Meet the demands of the hour." In other words, the past cannot be recalled. We have only the present in which to reveal God's love to others. Concentrate on spontaneous acts of kindness, willing acceptance of responsibilities, and especially an ever-ready witness that is adaptable and from the heart. As Peter so aptly put it, we must "always be prepared to give an answer to everyone who asks [us] to give the reason for the hope that [we] have. Do this with gentleness and respect ..." (1 Peter 3:15b-16a).

Third, after praying for (and receiving guidance in) our action, and being in a perpetual state of readiness to respond to whatever opportunities come our way, we must prepare for the inevitable conflict that will occur. Doing invariably involves conflict, especially doing what is right and helpful.

Biblical metaphors of the Christian life are battle words. Paul portrays us in a contest—a fight, a wrestling match, a race. Hear him as he declares, "For we wrestle not against flesh and blood, but against principalities, against powers, against the rulers of the darkness of this world, against spiritual wickedness in high places" (Eph. 6:12, KJV).

Again, the apostle to the Gentiles triumphantly states, at the close of his life: "I have fought the good fight, I have finished the race, I have kept the faith" (2 Tim. 4:7). For the terms *struggle* and

---

[89]The rendering *seize your opportunities* is provided by William Barclay. He offers this background and explanation: "The ancient manuscripts vary between two readings. (Romans 12:11b) Some read, 'Serve the Lord,' and some read 'Serve the time,' that is, 'Grasp your opportunities.'

"The ancient scribes used contractions in their writing. The most common words were always abbreviated. A common way of abbreviating was to leave out the vowels, as shorthand does, and to place a stroke along the top of the remaining letters. The word for 'Lord' is *Kurios*, and the term for 'time' is *kairos*. The abbreviation for both of these is *krs*. In th[is] section [that is] so filled with practical advice, it is more likely that Paul was saying to his people, 'Seize your opportunities as they come.'" William Barclay, *The Daily Study Bible: The Letter to the Romans*, 2nd ed. (Philadelphia: Westminster, 1957), pp. 178-79.

fight, Paul employs the Greek words *agon* and *agonizomai*. From these ancient terms we get our English words *agony* and *agonize*. Perseverance, suffering, and intense struggle are implied.

Timothy, who had a Greek father, was familiar with the Olympic Games, commonly referred to as *Agon*, "the noble agony." Therefore, he understood well when Paul exhorted him to "fight (*agonizomai*) the good fight of the faith" (1 Tim. 6:12). In other words, give your best to the one contest of eternal importance.

We must keep one thing in mind. The apostle Paul never employs the term *agon* in a negative way. Jim McKay on ABC's "Wide World of Sports" often referred to the "thrill of victory and the agony of defeat." But that's Jim McKay, not Paul. The agony that Paul alludes to is the opposite of defeat. Instead, it is the cry of victory: "I have agonized!"[90]

To opt for comfort rather than to agonize in the conflict that will inevitably occur in the excellent Christian's life is to lose sight of the One we serve. Jesus was the supreme combatant of satanic power. He is described by the writer of Hebrews as the One who "learned obedience from what he suffered" (5:8), the "author and perfecter of our faith, who for the joy set before him endured the cross, scorning its shame" (12:2).

We are invited to "consider him who endured such opposition from sinful men, so that [we] will not grow weary and lose heart" (12:3). In our day it is easy to lose sight of the real Jesus and to picture him as a synthetic, counterfeit Lord who neatly conforms to our hedonistic cravings. But be not deceived. This is not the Christ we serve.[91]

---

[90]Edward Kuhlman, "God's Strugglers in an Age of Video Sainthood," *His*, December 1983, p. 9.

[91]Kuhlman offers a dramatic statement concerning our tendency to take the easy way of inaction. As Judy Garland sang in "Somewhere Over the Rainbow," we see the world as a "giant lemon drop." Such a sugar-coated perspective is in sharp contrast to the one our Lord had. In Kuhlman's words: "Is a Christian one who having been found by Christ (the supreme battler of all satanic power) 'wraps the draperies of his couch about him and lies down to pleasant dreams'? Are we guilty of A. W. Tozer's indictment that because Christ did all the dying we think we can romp into heaven? Do we not feel the surge of struggle — the desire to enter the conflict — the true war?

Nor does an easy-going attitude characterize the "great cloud of witnesses" (12:1) spoken of by the author of Hebrews. Every one agonized in a fight against evil's powerful forces. But with God's all-wise and all-powerful guidance, they became truly excellent through obedience in action, in loving deeds, and in the midst of severe, unrelenting persecution.

We too must act in spite of the cost. Our witness cannot be tucked away in a warm and safe spot. It must be open, up front, and transparent—which means it will be vulnerable to Satan's weaponry. But with Christ—who endured the ultimate persecution for us—we will prevail. Not somehow. Triumphantly![92]

In no uncertain terms, God's Word commands us to join in the battle for truth. We must prepare our hearts by praying for fighting skills. We must alert our minds to opportunities so that we might respond immediately. We must expect plenty of opposition and struggle. It all adds up to a call to action!

What might we keep in mind as we wage our battle against Satan? Here are a few suggestions that might assist us.

A Ration Pack for Doers

Checklists can be helpful, particularly when you're embarking on a journey. And our Christian life is exactly that, a journey. Some reminders for those of us who are involved in godly, assertive action follow.

> There are no plateaus in the Christian life. We must move ahead in action in order to survive.[93] In effect, not to act is to retreat.

Struggle? The only struggle some people have is fitting the body into the snug designer jeans commercially cloned from fashion houses. We wear the world's brand on our hip pockets and wonder why we lack identity. Paul the struggler said: 'I bear on my body the marks of the Lord Jesus' (Gal. 6:17). The Lord's signature was Paul's identity, branded on his body. Elisabeth Elliot has rightly said that we will know who we are when we know whose we are. Designers don't determine identity. God does. And if we agonize, it will become clear when the victory is won." Ibid., p. 10.

[92]An inspirational book, *Not Somehow, But Triumphantly!*, was written by the late dean emerita of Eastern Nazarene College, Bertha Munro.

[93]The ancient Roman soldier typically wore a breastplate, leather straps to his thigh, sandals, helmet, and shinboards of cork and wood. But there was no protection in back, so that he would not be tempted to turn around in retreat. As

Doing must never take the place of being. As excellent Christians, we must excel in both (see the story of Mary and Martha, Luke 10:38-42).

We must lovingly do continuously. To await the big opportunity before acting is to lose valuable, fleeting opportunities to act in small ways.[94]

It is important that we distinguish between loving action and wheel-spinning busy work. The former increases, while the latter saps, spiritual energy.[95]

Actions, based on our convictions, must become increasingly independent of the reactions of others. God alone must become our guide.[96]

---

long as we march forward with deeds of loving action, we have spiritual protection.

[94]A God-directed act is never to be considered insignificant. It is much like the small finlike vortex blades on a giant aircraft. Although they are small in comparison to other parts of the plane, their function is crucial. They manufacture enough turbulence on a still day for landing. Concerning small things, Ed Young is right in declaring: "Think naughty a trifle, tho it small appear./Small sands make a mountain./Moments make a year, and trifles, life."

[95]Virginia Watts Smith, in "How Filling the Time with Good Activity Can Lead to Emptiness," confronts wheel-spinning busyness in the life of the Christian. Not recognizing Christ's lordship is one reason for living such an existence. In addition, she lists these problems: "(1) *Misinterpreting Scripture.* Not really understanding what Jesus meant when he said, 'I must be about my Father's business,' nor really knowing how to accomplish the work he wants us to do. (2) *Being insecure.* Thinking we must work hard and fast to get (and keep) the approval of God—and others. (3) *Believing we are indispensable.* 'If I don't do it, nothing will get done.' (4) *Somehow feeling infallible.* 'Oh, I couldn't do anything that wrong,' or 'I'm fine. Nothing will happen to me.' (5) *Being guilt-ridden.* 'I feel so guilty if I don't accomplish all the things he/she wants me to do.' (6) *Pride.* 'I'm important. Just look at all the things I accomplish,' or 'I can do it better.' (7) *False sense of values.* Temporal, not according to God's eternal values system. (8) *Improper use of time.* 'My time is really not my time. It belongs to God, and I will be accountable to him for use and misuse of this valuable commodity.' (9) *Martyr complex.* 'Well, if I die, I'll die working for God.' (10) *Trying to be perfect.* Paul, in Philippians 3:12 said, 'Not that I have already obtained in all this, or have already been made perfect ...' God has an ideal, certainly and wants us to work toward becoming that person he wants us to be. But God also wants us to be realistic. He knows we're human; after all, he created us. (11) *Not learning to say 'no.'* A definite weakness in many Christians. (12) *Selfish.* 'I want to do what I want to do, when I want to do it, how I want to do it, and no one is going to stop me.' (13) *Not learning to delegate.* Read Exodus 18. (14) *Becoming more concerned about quantity than quality."* Eternity, January 1981, p. 49.

[96]William McCumber, in an editorial entitled "Leadership Paradoxes," has listed ten conclusions about people in general. He found the latter in a newspaper

We must be aware of the numerous, rewarding derivatives of Christian action: self-confidence, lessening anxiety (It's better to do than stew), closer fellowship with Jesus and others, motivating others to act, and an increasing supply of God's grace.[97]

It must always be remembered that it is never too late for us to perform loving actions. Although opportunities might have been missed in the past, there are always other ones in the present.

The Time of Her Life

It is often difficult to see the far-reaching significance of our loving acts. We tend to be so caught up in the present.

---

article about Howard Ferguson, a wrestling coach, who initially formulated the list. "(1) People are illogical, unreasonable, and self-centered. Love them anyway. (2) If you do good, people will accuse you of selfish, ulterior motives. Do good anyway. (3) If you are successful, you win false friends and true enemies. Succeed anyway. (4) The good you do today will be forgotten tomorrow. Do good anyway. (5) Honesty and frankness make you vulnerable. Be honest and frank anyway. (6) The biggest men with the biggest ideas can be shot down by the smallest men with the smallest ideas. Think big anyway. (7) People favor underdogs, but follow only top dogs. Fight for a few underdogs anyway. (8) What you spend years building may be destroyed overnight. Build anyway. (9) People really need help, but may attack you if you do help them. Help them anyway. (10) Give the world the best you have and you'll get kicked in the teeth. Give the world the best you have anyway."

McCumber adds, "The news article called these Howard Ferguson's 'Paradoxical Commandments of Leadership.' They form … an interesting commentary upon our Lord's words: 'It is more blessed to give than to receive.' The value of an action lies, not in the response it will receive, but in the quality of the action itself. Doing what is right, because it is right and honors God, is abundantly worthwhile, whether or not it is understood, appreciated, or reciprocated." *Herald of Holiness*, 15 September 1982, p. 17.

[97]Daring to act does entail risk, but offers the potential for great dividends. For example, it has been found that it is more politically expedient to run for an office and lose than not to have run at all. By running you have attained some visibility.

A few years ago I made a list of ten risk-containing actions that I would pursue. I reasoned the chances were that I would be successful in five of them—which would not have occurred if I had done nothing. As for the five "failures," they only produce learning experiences for future trials. With a few midcourse corrections, they can eventuate in successes. In addition, there is the potential for "spin-offs" in relationship to the five successes. They can multiply, opening up other areas of opportunity and eventual success. All of this adds up to one conclusion: It is foolish not to try. There is too much potential for success.

Several years ago there were three junior-high-school girl friends who walked home from school together. As they walked, they usually discussed such things as the latest records, boyfriends, and clothing styles.

Two of the girls were sisters, one of whom would later become my wife. In contrast to the other girl, the sisters were Christians. And as Christians, they continuously sought opportunities to lead their friend Emily to Christ.

It was summer, and time for Christian youth camp at Santa Cruz. Emily was invited to go and she accepted. The other teenagers were sure to like her. She had beautiful red hair and the ability to say interesting things when she talked. In the junior high school she was popular and was known as "the brain."

Without Emily's knowledge, a gentleman in the church donated a large portion of her camp fee. It was the only way she could afford to go. In addition, the camp staff positions were filled by adults who lovingly volunteered their services. They sacrificed their time, knowing what a difference a Christian camp experience can mean in the lives of young people. And it did for Emily.

She became totally immersed in the various activities offered: athletic contests, crafts, and perhaps even a customary prank or two. But it was the time of her life for a more important reason. One evening, at the close of a soul-stirring message, her two friends noticed that the Holy Spirit's conviction had captured Emily's heart. They proceeded to discreetly invite her to give her life to Jesus. Her response was immediate. The three girls made their way to the altar to pray.

In a brief time, Emily looked up with a wide smile. The load of sin had been lifted. She had become a born-again Christian. The presence of God reigned supreme in her life. Everything would be different when she returned home.

The time to return came all too soon. Suitcases were packed and good-byes were said. All the way home they sang and recounted memories. Then it was home at last. The girls separated. The sisters went to their home and Emily went to hers. But they parted as Christians.

Involved in catching up with their summer chores, the sisters didn't have an opportunity to see their friend for a week or two.

Then one day they took a notion to stop by her house. Emily was in bed, and Emily's mother sadly informed them that she could not be disturbed.

Soon thereafter school started. But there was no Emily. Again the two sisters walked the four blocks to Emily's house. They were met by her grim-faced mother who invited them in. Then she spoke shocking words: "Girls, your friend Emily is going to die. She has a brain tumor."

Intense grief seized the girls. Not their friend Emily! It couldn't be. They were so close. They had shared so many wonderful times together. Surely she would get better. But she didn't. In a matter of days Emily died.

Her death, although tragic, did have a bright spot: she died a Christian. She would live with Jesus for eternity. Someday they would see their friend in heaven again. That fact was the only one that brought comfort to the hearts of the sisters.

God was able to transform Emily's life because his followers decided to act. Such actions made it possible for her to attend camp and experience life-changing fulfillment. One man provided the money. A pastor constantly encouraged the youth to attend. Volunteers sacrificially and effectively ran the camp program. And, yes, there were the two sisters. They refused to give up until their good friend had met their Best Friend face to face. A long chain of loving actions. A soul born into eternity!

Was it worth all the effort? Let's remember that question. Someday, in the not-too-distant future, we can ask Emily.

A Parting Word

If we are to escape hearing the siren call to excellence, we will be forced to withdraw from America, for our land is filled with the ringing sound.

Advertisers promise excellence. Politicians pretend to have it. Educators promote it. Athletes display it. Commercial slogans about excellence abound from sea to shining sea.

We're the mark of excellence. (General Motors)
Putting our energy into excellence. (Atlantic Richfield)
We deliver excellence 95,000 times a day. (Express Mail)

Seminars, conventions, and conferences focus on the theme. One former president established the Commission on Excellence in Education. Bearing the motto *Commitment to Excellence*, an N.F.L. team once won the Super Bowl.

But with excellence receiving such top billing, what ever happened to success? Is it removed from our consciousness and completely forgotten?

Far from it! Motivation to succeed is as strong as ever. It's just that excellence today is seen as the means of attaining it. If success is the onstage performance, excellence is the director who calls the shots behind the curtain.

Some declare that excellence as a means to success is an interim condition, and I hope they are right. May the day come when excellence is valued for itself. It is a standard that yields far-reaching, long-lasting, intrinsic reward. The ancient Greeks discovered this fact and thrived as a result.

But what does the issue of success versus excellence have to do with those of us who attempt to serve Jesus? Success, even as an interim goal, is a completely unscriptural motivation for our lives. Power, prestige, privilege, and wealth must not be given a place in our minds and affections. When we do possess them, they must be played down, generously shared, and continuously rededicated to the Master. Even a cursory reading of the Sermon on the Mount provides strong support for this position.

In contrast, biblical excellence *is* our mission. It is a legitimate standard with which to provide wise guidance for our lives. It is worthy of our utmost attention and deepest commitment.

Why is biblical excellence so valuable? It includes all the Christian virtues, but places the spotlight on *agape* love, the unconditional, God-breathed love. Therefore, for Christians, biblical excellence is not optional. It is essential. We accept it at the offset of our walk with God, and grow in it as we journey along the Christian way.

As such growth occurs, we will notice ourselves developing a Christ-like spirit. As my friend, the late Bill Draper, stated: "we become increasingly

> slow to suspect—quick to trust;
> slow to condemn—quick to justify;
> slow to offend—quick to defend;
> slow to expose—quick to shield;
> slow to belittle—quick to forbear;
> slow to provoke—quick to conciliate;
> slow to resent—quick to forgive."

We drift away from mediocrity. Our lives take on fulfillment and meaning, joy and peace. Our perspective becomes his perspective; our reward, his reward.

May we all hold high, and clutch tightly, the banner of Christian excellence. Today. Tomorrow. For eternity.

Then, a world that is attracted to secular excellence will increasingly come to embrace our kind of excellence, the excellence of authentic, divine love—placed in our hearts as a gift from God.

From the conscience that shrinks from new truth.

From the laziness that is content with half-truths.
From the arrogance that thinks it knows all truth.
Oh, God of truth, deliver us.

— Ancient Hebrew prayer

Appendix A

Trenton Spiritual Gifts Analysis

Introduction

Every Christian has received from the Holy Spirit a certain gift or gifts. As Paul states in Romans 12:6, "God has given each of us the ability to do certain things well." In this way, the Holy Spirit displays God's power through each of us as a means of building the entire church. It then becomes our Christian duty to put these gifts into action for the benefit of the Kingdom.

Before completing this analysis, you should understand four fundamental prerequisites for spiritual gift discovery. To definitely identify your spiritual gift(s) you must:

1. *Be a Christian.* You must be a committed member of the Body of Christ.
2. *Believe in Spiritual Gifts.* You must accept the fact that God has blessed you with one or more gifts.
3. *Be Willing to Work.* You must intend to do the job for which your spiritual gift(s) has equipped you. God will not show you your gift(s) just to satisfy your curiosity.
4. *Pray.* You must pray before, during, and after this process. Since God wants you to discover your gift(s), He certainly will guide and direct you as you attempt to identify them.

As you begin the process of discovering your spiritual gift(s), keep in mind that the results will show you how you are equipped to serve the Lord, helping to build up the church, the Body of Christ, to a position of strength and maturity ... to the point of being filled with Christ.

The Trenton Spiritual Gifts Analysis is an exercise designed to help give you a handle on what your spiritual gift(s) might be. It is adapted from a questionnaire that was originally created by Richard F. Houts (*Eternity*, May 1976, pp. 18-21) and later revised by C. Peter Wagner of Fuller Evangelistic Association. The Trenton version was first developed and used at Saint Paul Lutheran Church in Trenton, Michigan.

[To gain the full value of this exercise, you should use it in conjunction with more extensive teaching about spiritual gifts and/or under the guidance of your pastor or group leader. Additional copies of this questionnaire may be ordered from the Fuller Evangelistic Association, Box 989, Pasadena, California 91102.]

1. Go through the list of eighty-five statements on the Trenton Spiritual Gifts Analysis. For each one, say to yourself, "This statement has been experienced in my life ..." and then check the appropriate box: "Much," "Some," "Little," or "Not at All."
2. When you are finished, follow the directions for scoring the questionnaire.
3. Next, looking at the "Total" column of the Trenton Gifts Chart, enter below in the "Dominant" section the three gifts on which you received the highest scores. Then enter in the "Subordinate" section the next three highest-scoring gifts. This will give you a *tentative* evaluation of where your gifts may lie.

Dominant:

1._____

2._____

3._____

Subordinate:

1._____

2._____

3._____

Trenton Spiritual Gifts Analysis[98]

This statement has been satisfactorily experienced in my life:	Much (3)	Some (2)	Little (1)	Not at All (0)
1. Easily delegating important responsibilities to other people.				
2. Finding pleasure in the drawing and/or designing of various objects.				
3. Knowing that the repair and maintenance of things in my environment comes easily to me.				

This statement has been satisfactorily experienced in my life:	Much (3)	Some (2)	Little (1)	Not at All (0)
4. Leading other people to a decision for salvation through faith in Christ.				
5. Speaking words of encouragement to those who are troubled, discouraged, or not sure of themselves.				
6. Managing money well in order that I can give liberally to the				

[98]Copyright by Fuller Evangelistic Association, Box 989, Pasadena, California 91102. Used with permission. No further reprint authorization is granted.

work of the Lord.

7. Assisting key leaders to relieve them, so they can get back to their main job.

8. Providing food and/or lodging graciously and willingly to people who are in need.

9. Praying for other people and often losing track of the time.

10. Having the ability to discover new truths for myself.

11. Persuading other people to accomplish preset goals and objectives.

12. Working joyfully with and helping those people who are ignored by the majority of others around them.

13. Joyfully singing praises to God either alone or with other people.

This statement has been satisfactorily experienced in my life:	Much (3)	Some (2)	Little (1)	Not at All (0)
14. Being able to effectively play a musical instrument.				
15. Enjoying the fact that I am called on to do special jobs.				
16. Being able to help other people learn biblical facts and details which aid in the building up of their lives.				
17. Being able to formulate my thoughts and ideas into effective written forms.				
18. Having the ability to organize ideas, things, time, and people for more effective results.				
19. Finding joy in painting pic-				

tures or in other craft objects.

20. Working with various items manually and receiving enjoyment from it.

21. Sharing joyfully with other people how Jesus has brought me to Himself.

22. Enjoying the working out of complicated problems in other people's lives.

23. Giving my money liberally to the work of the Lord.

24. Helping in small ways that oftentimes seem to be behind the scenes.

This statement has been satisfactorily experienced in my life:	Much (3)	Some (2)	Little (1)	Not at All (0)

25. Enjoying having guests in my home.

26. Finding myself praying when I should be doing other things.

27. Knowing that the insights I possess and share with other people will bring changes in attitude and conviction to my fellow Christians.

28. Being able to lead other people toward the accomplishment of specified tasks.

29. Talking cheerfully with the elderly, the shut-in person, or those in jails or prisons.

30. Leading others in singing songs of praise to God or for pure enjoyment.

31. Being involved in a church, school, or local instrumental music presentation.

32. Enjoying routine work at

church that would seemingly
bore other people.
33. Enjoying the times I share my
knowledge, the knowledge of
others, and/or the love of
Christ with children and/or
adults.
34. Feeling secure in the fact that
the words I write will be of
benefit to those who read
them.

This statement has been satisfactorily experienced in my life:	Much (3)	Some (2)	Little (1)	Not at All (0)
35. Being able to work with facts and figures with positive results and personal satisfaction.				
36. Finding joy in lawn care and other outside maintenance.				
37. Enjoying the pleasures of the out-of-doors, gardening, land-scaping, and other projects.				
38. Enjoying meeting other people and sharing with them the joy and peace which Jesus and His love have given me.				
39. Being able to apply truth to my life effectively on a day-to-day basis, no matter what kind of crisis or conflict may arise.				
40. Feeling that I should give much to the Lord for all that He has done and is doing for me.				
41. Typing, filing, or recording figures or minutes for the Lord's work.				
42. Having guests and/or visitors in my presence and making them feel welcome and a part				

of things.

43. Feeling secure in the fact that my prayers continually work miracles in my life and in the lives of other people.

This statement has been satisfactorily experienced in my life:	Much (3)	Some (2)	Little (1)	Not at All (0)

44. Acquiring and mastering new facts and principles which can be applied to given situations to aid others in their growth and stability.

45. Knowing that others follow me and the examples I set because I have knowledge which contributes to the building of my church.

46. Visiting in hospitals and/or retirement homes and knowing that my presence has helped in comforting and cheering those people with whom I have come in contact.

47. Singing familiar Gospel songs alone or with groups of fellow Christians.

48. Utilizing my instrumental music talents for the appreciation of my friends and to the glory of God.

49. Feeling satisfaction in doing menial tasks for the glory of God.

50. Teaching children and/or adults about the love of Jesus and feeling that their faith is strengthened through my leadership.

This statement has been satisfactorily experienced in my life:	Much (3)	Some (2)	Little (1)	Not at All (0)
51. Composing and/or arranging newspaper or newsletter articles in an efficient, meaningful style.				
52. Planning and administering programs which will be of benefit to my fellow Christians.				
53. Enjoying the times that I am able to create beautiful items, especially when they benefit others.				
54. Finding that I enjoy maintaining and repairing things in my environment which others have not been good stewards of.				
55. Seeking out unbelievers in a continual manner in order to win them for Jesus.				
56. Being able to effectively counsel those people who are perplexed or confused, guilty or addicted.				
57. Feeling deeply moved when I am confronted with urgent financial needs in the work of God's Kingdom.				
58. Distributing tracts, Gospel literature, or other papers in my neighborhood and surrounding community.				

This statement has been satisfactorily experienced in my life:	Much (3)	Some (2)	Little (1)	Not at All (0)
59. Willing to open my home to guests and/or strangers and share with them what I have.				

60. Feeling that when I am asked to pray for others my prayers will have tangible results.

61. Reading and studying a great deal in order to build myself up in the understanding of biblical truths.

62. Being able to lead small or large groups of people in decision-making processes.

63. Helping other people with the knowledge that those whom I have helped will do little, if anything, in response to my action.

64. Finding much joy and pleasure in the seemingly simple routine of singing hymns and other Gospel selections.

65. Knowing that my ability to perform instrumental music has helped others grow has given me much satisfaction.

66. Willing to take orders rather than give them.

67. Presenting and discussing biblical stories with other people and feeling that those people will be edified through me and the power of the Word of God.

This statement has been satisfactorily experienced in my life:	Much (3)	Some (2)	Little (1)	Not at All (0)
68. Finding much pleasure in composing and writing paragraphs and stories for the edification of others.				
69. Being able to set goals and objectives and to make plans to reach and accomplish them.				

70. Finding that when I work with my hands at various arts and crafts, I derive much joy and satisfaction.

71. Knowing that the knowledge I have when it comes to building or repairing objects is of benefit to others gives me satisfaction.

72. Speaking to other people a message which is primarily the Gospel of salvation.

73. Choosing from several biblical alternatives an option which usually aids in comforting or directing other people.

74. Willing to maintain a lower standard of living in order to benefit God's work.

75. Finding joy in being an aide to someone who can utilize my help and concern.

76. Having the ability to make strangers, visitors, and guests feel at home when they are with me.

This statement has been satisfactorily experienced in my life:	Much (3)	Some (2)	Little (1)	Not at All (0)

77. Praying is one of my favorite spiritual exercises.

78. Knowing that I am able to distinguish key and important biblical truths and facts is beneficial to me and others as members of the Body of Christ.

79. Being able to motivate other people in a satisfactory, positive manner.

80. Comforting a fellow Christian during sickness or times of

problems and/or anxiety.

81. Singing is one of my favorite spiritual exercises.

82. Finding pleasure in playing a musical instrument either alone or with other people.

83. Enjoying it when others express a need for my help.

84. Sharing my knowledge of the love of Christ with children and/or adults in an effective and meaningful manner.

85. Knowing that my literary skill will aid other people and that they will be built up and informed because of it.

Trenton Gifts Chart

In the grid below, enter the numerical value of each of your responses next to the number of the corresponding statement.

Much = 3   Some = 2   Little = 1   Not at All = 0

Now add up the five numbers that you have recorded in each row, placing the sum in the "Total" column.

Rows	Value of Answers					Total	Gift
A	1	18	35	52	69	_____	Administration
B	2	19	36	53	70	_____	Craftsmanship (artistic)
C	3	20	37	54	71	_____	Craftsmanship (manual)
D	4	21	38	55	72	_____	Evangelism
E	5	22	39	56	73	_____	Exhortation-Wisdom
F	6	23	40	57	74	_____	Giving
G	7	24	41	58	75		

H	8	25	42	59	76	_____ Helps
I	9	26	43	60	77	_____ Hospitality
J	10	27	44	61	78	_____ Intercession
K	11	28	45	62	79	_____ Knowledge
L	12	29	46	63	80	_____ Leadership
M	13	30	47	64	81	_____ Mercy
N	14	31	48	65	82	_____ Music (vocal)
O	15	32	49	66	83	_____ Music (instrumental)
P	16	33	50	67	84	_____ Serving
Q	17	34	51	68	85	_____ Teaching
						_____ Writing

Review of Gift Definitions and Scripture References

The following pages contain *suggested* definitions of the spiritual gifts covered by this analysis. While not meant to be dogmatic, these definitions and their supporting Scriptures do correspond to characteristics of the gifts as expressed in the Trenton Spiritual Gifts Analysis.

A. Administration

The gift of administration is the special ability to understand clearly the immediate and long-range goals of a particular unit of the Body of Christ, and to devise and execute effective plans for the accomplishment of those goals.

Scriptural references: Prov. 24:3-4; Acts 6:1-7; 15:7-12; Rom. 12:8; 1 Cor. 12:5, 28; 1 Tim. 5:17

B, C. Craftsmanship

The gift of craftsmanship is the special ability to use your hands, thoughts, and mind to further the Kingdom of God through artistic or creative means. People with this gift may also serve as leaders for others in forming their abilities in this area. The gift may also be used in the areas of maintenance, care, and upkeep for the benefit and beautification of God's Kingdom here on earth.

Scriptural references: Exod. 30:22-25; 31:3-11; 2 Chron. 34:9-13; Acts 8:3; 16:14

D. *Evangelism*

The gift of evangelism is the special ability to share the Gospel with unbelievers in such a way that men and women become disciples of Jesus and responsible members of the Body of Christ.

Scriptural references: Acts 5:42; 8:5-6; 10:36; 11:20; 13:32; 21:8; Rom. 10:15; Eph. 4:11; 2 Tim. 4:5

E. *Exhortation-Wisdom*

The gift of exhortation-wisdom is the special ability to minister words of comfort, consolation, encouragement, and counsel to other members of the Body in such a way that they feel helped and uplifted. A person with this gift has insight and understanding of life situations which arise, perceiving what to do and how to do it.

Scriptural references: Acts 6:3-10; 14:22; Rom. 12:8; 1 Cor. 2:1-13; 12:8; 2 Cor. 9:2; 1 Tim. 4:13; Heb. 10:25; 2 Peter 3:15

F. *Giving*

The gift of giving is the special ability to contribute material resources to the work of the Lord with great joy, eagerness, and liberality.

Scriptural references: Mal. 3:10; Mark 12:41-44; Luke 18:12; Rom. 12:8; 2 Cor. 9:1-7; 9:2

G. *Helps*

The gift of helps is the special ability to invest one's talents in the life and ministry of other members of the Body, thus enabling the persons helped to increase their effectiveness in the use of their gifts.

Scriptural references: Mark 2:3-4; Acts 9:36; Rom. 16:1-2; 1 Cor. 12:18; 1 Tim. 6:2; 1 Peter 4:9-10

H. Hospitality

The gift of hospitality is the special ability to provide an open house and warm welcome for those in need of food and lodging, to care for those not in the immediate family with joy and effectiveness.

Scriptural references: Acts 16:15; 21:16-17; Rom. 12:9-13; 16:23; Heb. 13:1-2; 3 John 5-8

I. Intercession

The gift of intercession is the special ability to pray for extended periods of time on a regular basis, and also to see frequent and specific answers to one's prayers to a degree much greater than a fellow Christian who does not have an intercessory gift.

Scriptural references: Acts 12:1-17; 16:25-31; Col. 4:12; 1 Tim. 2:1-8; James 5:14-16

J. Knowledge

The gift of knowledge is the special ability to discover, accumulate, analyze, and clarify information and ideas that are pertinent to the growth and well-being of the Body.

Scriptural references: Rom. 15:14; 1 Cor. 12:8; 13:8

K. Leadership

The gift of leadership is the special ability to set goals in accordance with God's purpose for the future and to communicate these goals to others in such a way that they voluntarily and harmoniously work together to accomplish these goals for the glory of God.

Scriptural references: Acts 6:2-4; 7:10; 15:7-12; Rom. 12:8; Heb. 13:17

L. Mercy

The gift of mercy is the special ability to feel genuine concern and compassion for individuals, both Christian and non-Christian, who suffer distressing physical, mental, or emotional problems, and to translate that compassion into cheerfully done deeds that reflect Christ's love and alleviate their suffering.

Scriptural references: Luke 10:33-35; Acts 9:36; 16:33-34; Rom. 12:8; 1 Thess. 5:14

M, N. Music

The gift of music is the special ability to use one's voice in the singing of praises and joy to the Lord for the benefit of others or to play a musical instrument to the praise of the Lord and for the benefit of others.

Scriptural references: Deut. 31:22; 1 Sam. 16:16; 1 Chron. 16:41-42; 2 Chron. 5:12-13; 34:12

O. Serving

The gift of serving is the special ability to identify the unmet needs involved in a task related to God's work and to make use of available resources to meet those needs and help accomplish the desired goals.

Scriptural references: Luke 22:22-27; Rom. 12:7; 2 Cor. 8:19-29; 2 Tim. 1:16-18

P. Teaching

The gift of teaching is the special ability to communicate information relevant to the health and ministry of the Body and its members (children and/or adults) in such a way that they will learn and be edified.

Scriptural references: Acts 18:24-28; 20:20-21; Rom. 12:7; 1 Cor. 12:28; Eph. 4:11; 1 Tim. 3:2

Q. Writing

The gift of writing is the special ability to formulate thoughts and ideas into meaningful written forms so that the reader will find courage, guidance, knowledge, or edification through the words shared with him.

Scriptural references: Ps. 45:1; Acts 15:19-20; Phil. 3:1; 1 Tim. 3:14-15; Jude 3

Discovery of Your Spiritual Gifts

You have now just begun a process of discovering your spiritual gifts. As you reflect on the gifts you have tentatively identified through the Trenton Spiritual Gifts Analysis, try to discern which ones truly are or are not your gifts. To do so, follow this five-step approach.

Explore the possibilities. Read through the three key chapters in holy Scripture dealing with spiritual gifts (1 Cor. 12, Rom. 12, Eph. 4). Learn what the gifts are, what characterizes them, and how they function in the Body of Christ, so that you can have something concrete to look for as you move ahead.

Experiment with as many gifts as possible. The spiritual gifts analysis which you have just completed has helped you experiment with different gifts. Your feelings, reactions, and general outlook on the gifts were measured as you worked through the statements. Now you need to experiment further with the gifts you pinpointed in the analysis, i.e., the "dominant" and "subordinate" gifts. Unless you try the gifts this analysis has revealed, you will have a hard time knowing whether you really have them or not. Get involved in a ministry activity that will let you try out these gifts.

Examine your feelings. Since *God* has put the Body together, you will feel fulfilled when [you are] functioning in the proper area. Thus, if you enjoy your attempts to use a particular gift, that is a good sign that you possess that gift. If, however, you dislike the service activities associated with a certain gift, that is a fairly good sign that you do *not* have that gift.

Take time to examine your feelings regarding the gifts you identified through this questionnaire, both in the dominant and subordinate clusters. Are you comfortable with them? Do you feel that they are true reflections of yourself? Do you feel secure in the fact that you will be able to put your gifts to work in the Lord's Kingdom? Pray for the Holy Spirit's help and discernment as you examine your feelings concerning these gifts.

Evaluate your effectiveness. Since spiritual gifts are designed to benefit others, you should see positive results as you use your gift(s). If you do not see results when you experiment with a particular gift, you probably do not have that gift. But it could be that you do not give the gift a fair try, or that it will simply take time for you to learn to use the gift effectively. As you evaluate, pray for the courage to be honest with yourself and with your Lord.

Expect confirmation from the body. No gift can be discovered, developed, and used all on your own. Gifts are given to build up other members of the Body. If you have a gift, other Christians will recognize it and give you confirmation of it. If you feel that you have a particular gift but no one else agrees with you, then you should take a closer look at yourself and reevaluate.

And remember, in all these five steps, the key is prayer. The Lord will lead you to accurate discoveries of your gift(s) if you allow Him to guide and direct you in all your endeavors.

Appendix B

Temperament Test

The realization of excellence in our lives is actualized through the human vessel that God has given us. Thus, at the offset, we must comprehend who we are—and that, certainly, includes our psychological tendencies. We must understand our unique temperament, along with its strengths and vulnerabilities.

The Greek philosopher and physician Hippocrates (400 B.C.), identified four basic temperament types: sanguine, choleric, melancholic, and phlegmatic. Twentieth-century psychologist Karl Jung formulated four similar types: extrovert feeling type (sanguine); extrovert thinking type (choleric); introvert thinking type (melancholic); and introvert feeling type (phlegmatic).

Recently the four types have been popularized by Tim F. LaHaye[99]. Florence Littauer, after reading LaHaye's books, lectured on the four temperaments throughout North America.[100]

The following descriptions are not precise, nor do all of the characteristics apply to everyone in every case. We are each a unique blend of the traits. Nevertheless, most of us tend to have one temperament or another.

Sanguines are optimistic, verbose storytellers. They're the "live wires" at parties—emotional, enthusiastic, animated, bubbling with cheer. Such persons make friends easily and love people. They are spontaneous, do not hold grudges, and thrive on compliments.

---

[99]Tim F. LaHaye, *Spirit-Controlled Temperament* (Wheaton: Tyndale House, 1966), *Understanding the Male Temperament: What Every Man Would Like to Tell His Wife about Himself...But Won't* (Old Tappan, NJ: Revell, 1977), and *Transformed Temperaments* (Wheaton: Tyndale House, 1971).

[100]Florence Littauer, *Personality Plus* (Old Tappan, NJ: Revell, 1982).

On the negative side, sanguines crave popularity and being the center of attention. If there is credit to be given, they want it. Often such individuals dominate conversations, fail to listen to others, and interrupt. Sanguines frequently exaggerate, dwell on trivia, and seldom remember names. Their loud voices and laughter can alienate those to whom they appear phony or egotistical. Finally, they are quick to get angry and often seem childish.

Cholerics, like sanguines, are extroverts and optimistic. However, their primary goal is to get things done. They are action people, strong-willed, decisive, confident. Hence, they are leaders — getting things (and people) organized, making changes, and righting wrongs.

They're often perceived as being bossy, impatient, quick-tempered, and under stress. They are competitive and poor losers. They love controversy, are inflexible and unsympathetic, and offer few compliments.

Melancholics are deep, thoughtful people. Many are talented, creative, and gifted in music or art. Others love detail work: graphs, charts, figures — the components of research analysis. Melancholics are sensitive to others, self-sacrificing, and conscientious.

Negatively, such individuals tend to see the dark side of life. They can easily become moody and depressed because they focus too much on themselves and their feelings.

Phlegmatics are introverts and pessimists who would rather observe than participate. They have few enemies because they're casual, relaxed, cool. In addition, they are well-balanced, consistent, and quiet. Although they keep their emotions hidden, phlegmatics are mostly sympathetic and kind.

On the other hand, phlegmatics can be so low-key they appear unenthusiastic and boring. At times their laid-back exterior masks worries and fears. Often they are indecisive, making them the last to volunteer for responsibilities. Although they seem easy-going, at times they are hiding a stubborn, selfish streak.

To summarize, think of the four types in these ways:

Sanguines: Happy, chatty, forgetful.
Cholerics: Leaders, drivers, dominating.
Melancholics: Thinkers, perfectionists, sensitive.
Phlegmatics: Calm, easy-going, indecisive.[101]

The Temperament Test

This word-association test was developed by Florence and Fred Littauer and has been used with thousands of participants in their "Personality Plus" seminars. In each of the following rows of four words across, place an X in front of the *one word* that *most often applies* to you. Be sure to mark one word on each line, even if, in some cases, the choices do not fit you exactly. From each set of four words, pick the one that *comes closest* to describing you. Instructions on how to score the test follow.

1____Animated	____Adventurous	____Analytical	____Adaptable
2____Persistent	____Playful	____Persuasive	____Peaceful
3____Submissive	____Self-sacrificing	____Sociable	____Strong-willed
4____Considerate	____Controlled	____Competitive	____Convincing
5____Refreshing	____Respectful	____Reserved	____Resourceful
6____Satisfied	____Sensitive	____Self-reliant	____Spirited
7____Planner	____Patient	____Positive	____Promoter
8____Sure	____Spontaneous	____Scheduled	____Shy
9____Orderly	____Obliging	____Outspoken	____Optimistic
10____Friendly	____Faithful	____Funny	____Forceful
11____Daring	____Delightful	____Diplomatic	____Detailed
12____Cheerful	____Consistent	____Cultured	____Confident
13____Idealistic	____Independent	____Inoffensive	____Inspiring

---

[101]Based on information from Fritz Ridenour, *What Teenagers Wish Their Parents Knew About Kids* (Waco: Word, 1982).

14___Demonstrative	___Decisive	___Dry humor	___Deep
15___Mediator	___Musical	___Mover	___Mixes easily
16___Thoughtful	___Tenacious	___Talker	___Tolerant
17___Listener	___Loyal	___Leader	___Lively
18___Contented	___Chief	___Chartmaker	___Cute
19___Perfectionist	___Permissive	___Productive	___Popular
20___Bouncy	___Bold	___Behaved	___Balanced
21___Brassy	___Bossy	___Bashful	___Blank
22___Undisciplined	___Unsympathetic	___Unenthusiastic	___Unforgiving
23___Reluctant	___Resentful	___Resistant	___Repetitious
24___Fussy	___Fearful	___Forgetful	___Frank
25___Impatient	___Insecure	___Indecisive	___Interrupts
26___Unpopular	___Uninvolved	___Unpredictable	___Unaffectionate
27___Headstrong	___Haphazard	___Hard to please	___Hesitant
28___Plain	___Pessimistic	___Proud	___Permissive
29___Angered easily	___Aimless	___Argumentative	___Alienated
30___Naive	___Negative attitude	___Nervy	___Nonchalant
31___Worrier	___Withdrawn	___Workaholic	___Wants credit
32___Too sensitive	___Tactless	___Timid	___Talkative
33___Doubtful	___Disorganized	___Domineering	___Depressed
34___Inconsistent	___Introvert	___Intolerant	___Indifferent
35___Messy	___Moody	___Mumbles	___Manipulative
36___Slow	___Stubborn	___Show-off	___Skeptical
37___Loner	___Lord over others	___Lazy	___Loud
38___Sluggish	___Suspicious	___Short-tempered	___Scatterbrained
39___Revengeful	___Restless	___Reluctant	___Rash
40___Compromising	___Critical	___Crafty	___Changeable

Scoring Instructions

To score the Temperament Test, transfer your marks from the preceding pages to this sheet, add up your strengths and weaknesses, and combine both sets of totals to see which temperaments are the strongest.

Strengths			
Sanguine	**Choleric**	**Melancholic**	**Phlegmatic**
1_____Animated	_____Adventurous	_____Analytical	_____Adaptable
2_____Playful	_____Persuasive	_____Persistent	_____Peaceful
3_____Sociable	_____Strong-willed	_____Self-sacrificing	_____Submissive
4_____Convincing	_____Competitive	_____Considerate	_____Controlled
5_____Refreshing	_____Resourceful	_____Respectful	_____Reserved
6_____Spirited	_____Self-reliant	_____Sensitive	_____Satisfied
7_____Promoter	_____Positive	_____Planner	_____Patient
8_____Spontaneous	_____Sure	_____Scheduled	_____Shy
9_____Optimistic	_____Outspoken	_____Orderly	_____Obliging
10_____Funny	_____Forceful	_____Faithful	_____Friendly
11_____Delightful	_____Daring	_____Detailed	_____Diplomatic
12_____Cheerful	_____Confident	_____Cultured	_____Consistent
13_____Inspiring	_____Independent	_____Idealistic	_____Inoffensive
14_____Demonstrative	_____Decisive	_____Deep	_____Dry humor
15_____Mixes easily	_____Mover	_____Musical	_____Mediator
16_____Talker	_____Tenacious	_____Thoughtful	_____Tolerant
17_____Lively	_____Leader	_____Loyal	_____Listener
18_____Cute	_____Chief	_____Chartmaker	_____Contented
19_____Popular	_____Productive	_____Perfectionist	_____Permissive
20_____Bouncy	_____Bold	_____Behaved	_____Balanced

Totals_____   _____   _____   _____

Weaknesses			
Sanguine	Choleric	Melancholic	Phlegmatic
21____Brassy	____Bossy	____Bashful	____Blank
22____Undisci-plined	____Unsym-pathetic	____Unfor-giving	____Unenthu-siastic
23____Repeti-tious	____Resistant	____Resentful	____Reluctant
24____Forgetful	____Frank	____Fussy	____Fearful
25____Interrupts	____Impatient	____Insecure	____Indecisive
26____Unpre-dictable	____Unaffec-tionate	____Unpopular	____Unin-volved
27____Haphaz-ard	____Head-strong	____Hard to please	____Hesitant
28____Permis-sive	____Proud	____Pessimistic	____Plain
29____Angered easily	____Argumen-tative	____Alienated	____Aimless
30____Naive	____Nervy	____Negative attitude	____Nonchalant
31____Wants credit	____Workaholic	____Withdrawn	____Worrier
32____Talkative	____Tactless	____Too sensitive	____Timid
33____Disor-ganized	____Domi-neering	____Depressed	____Doubtful
34____Inconsis-tent	____Intolerant	____Introvert	____Indifferent
35____Messy	____Manipu-lative	____Moody	____Mumbles
36____Show-off	____Stubborn	____Skeptical	____Slow
37____Loud	____Lord over others	____Loner	____Lazy
38____Scatter-brained	____Short-tempered	____Suspicious	____Sluggish
39____Restless	____Rash	____Revengeful	____Reluctant
40____Change-able	____Crafty	____Critical	____Compro-mising

Totals_____   _____   _____   _____

Combined
Totals_____   _____   _____   _____

Appendix C

Survey of Christian Scholars and Leaders (Second Edition)

Participants:

Mark O. Hatfield, politician
Martin Marty, author and educator
Charles W. Colson, author
Russ Spittler, educator
David A. Hubbard, former administrator and educator
Fritz Ridenour, author
Jim Spruce, pastor
Neil Strait, administrator
Stephen Nease, administrator
John Walvoord, educator
Dale Evans Rogers, entertainer and author
Ted Engstrom, administrator and author
M. Norvel Young, administrator
William S. Banowsky, administrator
Dan Boone, pastor
Stephen Manley, evangelist
F. LaGard Smith, educator and author
Neil B. Wiseman, educator and author
Gordon Wetmore, administrator
Millard Reed, administrator

Question #1   Why does "excellence" persist as a theme in Christian books, conferences, etc.?

"Christ said, in the Sermon on the Mount, '*Be perfect, therefore, as your heavenly Father is perfect.*' Suffice it to say, this is a powerful command. In many ways, the whole Sermon on the Mount is a call to perfection. Christ's words sharply invite us to another standard, a heavenly standard. I cannot help but cry to myself as I read it, 'But Lord, help me, for I cannot be perfect'!

"Christ is quick to answer. His death on the cross makes my faith, not my perfection, a condition for salvation. Knowing this, am I to strive to live any less excellently? Remember James who wrote, '*What good is it, my brothers, if a man claims to have faith but has no deeds? Can such faith save him?*' In other words, believing in the saving grace of Christ on the cross and seeking to live a life of excellence simply cannot be separated.

"Therefore, is it any surprise that the theme of so many Christian sermons, books and conferences is that of equipping us to live a life of Christian excellence? For Christians responding to God's love by seeking to walk in His will, nothing could be more relevant. What better reward would there be than upon meeting your Maker face-to-face, hearing, '*Well done, my good and faithful servant.*'" (Mark O. Hatfield)

"Pope Pius XII once said that we should thank God that He has placed us in such a crisis moment; it is not permitted any Christian any longer to be mediocre. Hence, reaching for excellence is part of the call. On the other hand, I think we Christians often sense that in a secular-pluralist world we naturally would come in second or would carry a handicap. So we have to work twice as hard to show excellence in our days and ways. Finally, the pursuit of excellence (Phil. 4) is an intrinsic goal of the life in Christ." (Martin Marty)

"The reason that this is so necessary today is that the world has divorced faith and life. It's perfectly alright to believe whatever we choose to believe as long as we do not let it affect the way we think about politics, law, art, science. We can argue all we want apologetically, that science cannot be sustained apart from the rational world order which Christianity provides, but we're less likely to persuade the other side by apologetics than by demonstrating excellence on the part of our own scientists." (Charles W. Colson)

"Excellence seems to be a wistful dream of an expiring culture. With moral decay on every hand, in all sectors of society, there emerges a pining for what's right and best and good. But it's illusive. So now it's the subject of seminars and books. Those best at it may be unconscious of it—Hutterite Brethren Communities, aging rural craftspersons, and the like." (Russ Spittler)

"(It is because excellence is such a pervasive theme in God's Word). Ps. 8 *'How excellent is your Name, O Lord.'* All true excellence flows from the Person (Name) of God. Without this Source, excellence becomes a synonym for efficiency. Wasn't it James O'Toole who cautioned pastors by saying: 'Excellence is the enemy of greatness'? Have a look at Phil. 1:10, 4:8, 2 Pet. 1:3, Is. 28:29, Dan. 5:12, 14; 6:3, Rom. 2:18. And above all excellence equals love in 1 Cor. 12:31." (David A. Hubbard)

"Some want to serve the Savior well, and excellence is their goal; others are earning their salvation and they confuse excellence with perfectionism." (Fritz Ridenour)

"Excellence is more a characteristic shaped by personality, culture and our times, than a biblical mandate. We are driven by competition, the fear of failure and personal reward to look good.

We need to excel.... Excellence surely is the goal over success."
(Jim Spruce)

"There is a desire/hunger built into each person to strive for
the best, to stretch to a higher standard to attain.... Each person
is endowed with this hunger by Creator-God.

"Excellence persists because it is an area which eludes people. They are constantly seeking ways to discover/attain
excellence. Some think it is utopia, hence, the search. In a world
where so much is out-of-control, the human mind/heart hungers
for a principle, some integrity, some model to challenge the evil
and give hope." (Neil Strait)

"Contrary to a secular definition of excellence, i.e., adherence
to a pattern or guidelines that result in profit or prominence,
Christian excellence may be defined as conforming to the pattern
established by Jesus Christ. An adequate expression of His love is
the 'summum bonum' of Christian excellence. Thus, the trend
continues because the quest for this kind of excellence is a scriptural command. (Jn. 15:12-13)" (Stephen Nease)

"In our modern world, it is increasingly necessary to have
quality and excellence in all that is done. It is only natural that
Christians should have this high standard in relation to all their
activities ... 1 Thes. 5:23. We are exhorted to be *'blameless.'* 2 Thes.
1:12. The standard is stated that the Lord Jesus Christ may be
glorified in us ... Col. 3:17. *'Whatever you do in word or deed, do it
all in the name of the Lord Jesus.'* Col. 3:23. *'Whatever you do, do it
heartedly, as unto the Lord not to man.'* Col. 4:6. *'Let your speech
always be with grace.'* It should be abundantly clear that the
Scriptures in numerous instances exhort us to a high standard of
excellence in morality and performance and in standards of conduct." (John F. Walvoord)

"Today, the world is judging Christians — In trying to gain the favor of the world, Christians are not taking a firm stand on morality. Many of us are afraid of offending the nonbelievers, and ... are straddling the fence on vital issues." (Dale Evans Rogers)

"(It persists) Probably because the concept of 'excellence' has been increasingly neglected in our secular society. And — when transcendent truth is scorned, or at best neglected, the idea of excellent performance is minimized." (Ted Engstrom)

"It is often assumed that Christian people are not demanding of themselves or others — permissive academically and tend to want to substitute goodness for excellence. To substitute negatives (prohibitions) for active efforts." (M. Norvel Young)

"Because Christ said, '*Ye shall be perfect as your heavenly Father is perfect.*' This, obviously, is the very highest possible calling to the most exacting standards of excellence in our personal lives, families, professional careers, and service to mankind. We may not ever attain perfection, but we must never cease striving." (William S. Banowsky)

"Part of the persistence is due to fallenness. There is a worldly side of all of us that wants to be impressed, wowed, amazed. The church is competing with the gods of the world for the devotion of people — and people are drawn to excellence. Like sex-food-art, etc., everything good that can be biblically excellent can also be twisted into a flesh-based excellence that is hollow." (Dan Boone)

"There is such a low level of Christian experience, in this hour, that a hunger has been created for something beyond." (Stephen Manley)

"In an age of egalitarian mediocrity, people know, deep down, that excellence is a better way than blind conformity. To excel—to be excellent—means standing out from the crowd as an individual who dares to be different. Who dares to defy the conventions of normalcy. Who rises above the ever-lowering expectations of a devalued cultural currency." (F. LaGard Smith)

"… because so many of us long to see (excellence) in ourselves and others. Too much of Christian performance—thinking, speaking and writing in Christian circles is less—much less—than it could be.

"Excellence is a common quest because of the One whom we serve. In His modeling we see so much of what we want to be and so much of what we have not yet become. How can we give Him less than our best? Excellence is a common quest because we believe the Lord Christ is worthy of our best.

"Excellence is fulfilling our mission in the world in the most competent, committed way possible. It is to be judged in a person's inmost parts where only God and the individual know what is happening.

"Personally, I think of excellence as a moving target that shapes me more and more into Christlikeness, something like humility and wisdom. About the time I think I have excellence, humility and wisdom, I have lost the meaning of the terms and the power these ideas create in shaping me into Christlikeness." (Neil B. Wiseman)

"It still persists in Christian books and conferences because it is still a relevant item. There may be synonyms such as integrity and ethical commitment which may be carrying similar freight." (Gordon Wetmore)

Question #2 What special forms, or expressions, of Christian excellence are called for in the 90s — given the conditions of the world and church?

"If only this question (were) asked more often. For the most part, the special forms of Christian excellence called for by the early church are called for today. The Great Commission is our commission and the need to see God as sovereign has remained constant.

"As God calls individuals to become regenerate, and as He becomes the center of their lives, self-centeredness is replaced by other-centeredness. Today and in the past, this conversion has been reflected in the fruit of the Spirit: love, joy, peace, patience, kindness, goodness, faithfulness, gentleness and self-control. This is Christian excellence in its purest form, and it has always had a tremendous impact on our souls, in our churches and in our communities.

"The onslaught of modernity calls us to be discerning in a special way. As a United States Senator, I witness the politicization of Christian principles. This is potentially dangerous. Too often, in the political realm and elsewhere, the wisdom and power of God is replaced with the wisdom and power of modernity.

"I am reminded of 1 Corinthians, where Paul writes, *'Where is the wise man? Where is the scholar? Where is the philosopher of this age? Has not God made foolish the wisdom of the world? For since in the wisdom of God the world through its wisdom did not know him, God was pleased through the foolishness of what was preached to save those who believe.'* Today, we are called to resolutely discern between the world's wisdom, which centers our minds almost without effort, and God's wisdom, which has the power to save." (Mark O. Hatfield)

"We have to 'outthink' someone or other. While we may have deficiencies on the 'good works' front, we are further behind on the 'great thoughts' horizon. These are exciting days to do Christian thinking, as other systems of thought and society implode. But no one will sit still for mediocrity." (Martin Marty)

"I have the feeling that Christians do Christian things very, very well (e.g., biblical exegesis, hermeneutics, church growth/ development). This is as it should be. We should do things with excellence in the pursuit of spiritual growth.

"But, we should do things with excellence in all areas of life, not just in matters Christian. On this score, I think we evangelicals have fallen woefully short.

"I'm reminded that Bach produced magnificent music and always signed the musical scores SDG, Sola Deo Gloria. He pursued excellence in his calling, that is music, but in doing so knew that he was glorifying God." (The same was true of Handel and Dostoyesky, with their beautiful works that reflected obvious Christian messages.)

"I'm reminded also that the guilds in the Middle Ages were formed by Christian craftsmen. (Here were persons who) held themselves out to be producers of the highest quality products.

"Os Guinnes quite correctly makes the point that during the Reformation the first thing that people were disciplined in was their vocation so that whatever they undertook, they would do so to the glory of God. This was considered integral to their witness as indeed it should be today.

"When the secular world reads Christian literature that maybe contains a good message but is bad literature, it does not glorify God. I think we should constantly strive to elevate our standards to produce things better than they are produced in the secular world precisely because it is our witness to do things to the glory of God with excellence." (Charles W. Colson)

"Try simple personal virtues: promptness, reliability, promise-keeping. It's easy to etch larger cultural needs, but none will work without well-cultivated personal virtues." (Russ Spittler)

"See Micah 6:8. Also, any Christian who is a member of a local body should make his commitment to that body a matter of excellence. The church is not a matter of "been there, done that." As the pace of living increases at light speed, there is less and less time for everything and church often gets short shrift. To be excellent church members we must "be there, doing that" every week." (Fritz Ridenour)

"(1) Church architecture. Even if plain, young couples and mothers will continue to expect decent nursery and bathroom conditions. (2) Integrity. There will be absolutely no tolerance for moral or ethic misconduct. (3) Church services. People continue to want worship that connects with real life, that is meaningful and clear." (Jim Spruce)

"I think the truest expression(s) are the biblical admonitions, which not only address the thirst for excellence, but the world issues as well. These, in their truest forms, are principles which call life to excellence.

"The truest expression of excellence is articulated through the life of that individual whose personal mission is principle-based, and whose life is lived out in the arena, courageously and even aggressively, fulfilling the personal mission." (Neil Strait)

"Christians need to learn to express Christ's love firmly and openly—but without such extremes as those who kill abortion doctors, etc.! (Stephen Nease)

"In our modern world, Christian morality is the exception rather than the rule, and Christians should be beyond reproach Even as Paul expressed in 1 Thess. 4:12, our testimony should be good *'toward those who are outside,'* that is the world. Again in Phil. 4:5 we are exhorted to *'Let your gentleness be known to all men.'*" (John F. Walvoord)

"One of the great barriers of attaining excellence ... is our (neglect) of the Word of God. (We are too time-conscious). We do not take the time to listen to God during our meditation. He speaks in the small voice inside us when we are quiet from the world. There are many siren voices from the world, clamoring for our attention, and we need to shut everyone out of our hearts and minds, and 'be still and know that (He is) God.'" (Dale Evans Rogers)

"The beginning of the call should be in the home — and with parenting. It should be constantly enforced in and through the church — from the pulpit, in classes, through small groups and by other means." (Ted Engstrom)

"First, moral and ethical excellence ... (Then,) being willing to use technology effectively, be intellectually disciplined, develop financial skills to support Christian values in benevolence, etc. Hard work is demanded in Christian areas — scholarly writing, lecturing, administrating, teaching." (M. Norvel Young)

"In two expressions: (1) Our understanding of the Christian faith and our communication of it to the world. This must include the most rigorous scholarship, an academic openness, a courageous trust in God rather than a fearful clinging to our own provincial system. (2) In (the) world-class professional excellence — business, law, government, politics, academic achievement." (William S. Banowsky)

"I am cut to the bone by the Word of God in these days concerning the (overemphasis on) 'doing' among us. We cannot think of a church existing without doing. We are afraid to (cease) 'doing.' How would we ever survive? However, the opposite of doing is not inactivity; it is being. (We must) be the will of God. It is great to cease to preach, and actually be(come), the sermon.... The New Testament is filled with this emphasis, which means there is only one 'excellence.' It is Him. If we would let Him be what He is in our world, we would experience 'excellence' again. But, we are always manipulating, pulling string, controlling, and the result is always a cheap copy of the real thing.

"We have proven in the 90s (that) we are not adequate for the challenges before us. I don't know why we don't quit and let Him do what He has always wanted to do." (Stephen Manley)

"In a world that demands rights, the excellence of responsibility; in a world of sexual license, the excellence of purity; in a materialistic world, the excellence of contentment; in a church of accommodation, the excellence of doctrinal integrity; in a church of entertainment, the excellence of piety; in a church of social status, the excellence of service." (F. LaGard Smith)

"I believe excellence of character is among our most pressing issues. Concerns like integrity, openness, honesty, forthrightness, rejecting shallow image-building, self-awareness, and attacking so much 'goof dust' in thought and publishing all need attention.

"... Personal spiritual formation is an area where excellence is needed. How does one become a fit vessel for service and useful to Christ and the cause? How is excellence different for the pre-retiree vs. the mid-life person?" (Neil B. Wiseman)

(Integrity and ethical commitment.) "In addition the issue of respect for diversity ... The issues relating to collaboration of evangelical movements around central Christian doctrines will continue to be relevant into the 21st century. The 'young fogies,' as characterized by Tom Oden, represent insurgences of interest in essential Christianity which predate the controversies of the fifteenth through twentieth centuries.

"A case can be made that in the face of growing world religions Christian groups are finding common grounds upon which they may express their discipleship in all forms of life. The fresh visions that are being brought by growing Christian groups in the continents of Africa and South America could bring fresh life to the (U.S.) Christian movement. I look forward with anticipation to new expressions of the Christian faith in these 'unspoiled' Christian movements.

"Another set of initiatives for the Christian faith will have to do with the growing interest in religion in the public square. It will be interesting to see how politicians will come out of the closet re: morality issues in the 1996 race." (Gordon Wetmore)

"... in a highly competitive society, it seems important that each of us exceed the quality level of our brother and sister ... Deming focused on the word 'quality'—his emphasis being that each person within a given team could practice top quality, or conversely, an individual might 'excel' in a climate of low achievement and still not do well.

"All this becomes a moot point in the light of our conversation on holiness. And sometimes the current talk on holiness seems to be couched much more in effort terms than in grace terms ..." (Millard Reed)

Question #3 What person, living today, would you select as most reflecting the biblical meaning/practice of excellence? Please share the basis for your choice.

"I can think of no one in the 20th century who has had a greater impact as an evangelist than Billy Graham. Mother Teresa continues to have a profound career, serving Christ as she serves others. Carl Henry, founding editor of *Christianity Today*, and author of numerous books, has made incredible contributions to theological thought. With their respective abilities to evangelize, serve and study, these three have typified Christian excellence, and I hesitate to choose one over the other." (Mark O. Hatfield)

"Pastor Beyers Naude of South Africa, the (white) Reformed pastor who showed stirrings of conscience to do an about face; to represent the white community as no one else did in times of change; to be an eloquent minister of the Gospel; to keep a right spirit in the midst of meanness." (Martin Marty)

"Colin Powell and David Alan Hubbard. (Forgive the chauvinism!) Both combine integrity, competence, independence, wide admiration. Both are quiet but effective leaders." (Russ Spittler)

"My wife. She is a daily witness and model of Christian love and caring." (Fritz Ridenour)

"Probably Henri Nouwen, Catholic priest, who walked away from very much and now serves as a counselor in a home for mentally challenged people. I believe he has helped me to see that to be 'good and faithful' may have been our highest goal after all. He embodies the concept of servanthood ..." (Jim Spruce)

"Billy Graham ... His stature and opportunity to voice among his peers, plus opportunities to counsel leaders, has established him as a model of integrity. Mother Teresa is another, whose simple life gives evidence of excellence." (Neil Strait)

"Billy Graham. Esther Sanger." (Stephen Nease)

"Billy Graham and Mother Teresa." (Ted Engstrom)

"Robert Jones, Duke Medical School heart surgeon, (has) clear Christian motivation to know and give best skills to God's glory." Doris Clark, Director of Medical Center in mountains near Tegucigalpa, Honduras—great administrator, servant leader, sacrificial, self-denying, tireless worker, Christian. David Davenport rigorous in his own life, disciplined, productive, unusually good administrator. Demands much of himself and coworkers. Not willing to settle for second best. His priorities are right: Christian commitment personally, family devotion— including time for them." (M. Norvel Young)

"Billy Graham, Mother Teresa, James Dobson, Charles Colson. I pick these types because they are actually in the arena and are very widely respected by Christians and millions of others. (Concerning Billy Graham) Who else in America could have gone to Oklahoma City with the prestige and respect to convey the blessings of God on the suffering families ...?" (William S. Banowsky)

"Chuck Colson: authentic, thinking, compassion expressed in tangible ministry. Paul Snellenberger, local grade school principal—everything he does is with excellence of character and spirit." (Dan Boone)

"All of the 'worthy women' who have defied feminist propaganda and daily sacrifice themselves on behalf of the next generation in the behind-the-scenes, often unappreciated task of child-rearing." (F. LaGard Smith)

"Chuck Colson and Phillip Yancey. This is a hard call because so many followers of Christ are excellent in one or two phases of their lives and ministry, and so obviously lacking in others.

"... many of our brothers and sisters are excellent. I think many unknown and unheralded people are excellent in so much of their lives." (Neil B. Wiseman)

"It is difficult to name a single living person who most reflects the biblical meaning and practice of excellence. Billy Graham will get a great number of votes. Mother Teresa will have a strong group of supporters. I, for one, would also give some votes to Jimmy Carter. In support of the last nomination I would site [sic] his strong insistence, while in office, in attempting to be a Christian. Since his active presidency he has been a model of activity in helping the homeless and attempting to bring a moderate position to the recent tensions within the Baptist Church.

"I think, Jon, I would want to draft a kind of composite, something like a Christian everyman, to represent the strong silent pervasive presence of Christians who faithfully maintain the life of the Kingdom ... it could be that when the records are reviewed the resurgencies of the lay movement could be one of the greatest representations of Christian excellence in the last quartile of the twentieth century." (Gordon Wetmore)

Appendix D

Leader's Guide

GETTING STARTED

An Important Word To The Teacher

This *Leader's Guide* should assist you in presenting each lesson creatively and with positive results. Remember that this guide is a resource that suggests a variety of helpful methods to accomplish your goals.

Realizing that the lecture method often has a negative impact on potential learners, our basic approach centers around student participation. In addition, such participation is not limited to thinking, writing, speaking, and feeling in the classroom. You will discover that the lessons include exercises to be done during the week. Experience is, perhaps, the best teacher.

As the leader, please be reminded of the following points:

1. Keep the Word of God at the center of your lesson delivery. It is easy to drift into an exchange of opinion that leads to pooled ignorance and needless conflict. That is counter-productive.

2. Do not feel obligated to use all of the suggestions offered for each session. Pick and choose, depending on the needs of your unique situation. Hopefully, in addition to the ones offered, you will generate some creative approaches of your own.

3. Be aware of the fact that there is an overlap of subjects throughout the book. *Excellence* is an umbrella term that covers many areas discussed. Realizing this, attempt to limit drift in discussion. Restrict your focus to the specific topics highlighted — otherwise, you may use up the book prematurely and seriously diminish the overall effect.

4. Feel free to encourage disagreement with author's conclusions. For example, he may point out conclusions from a particular angle of thought. Have your class consider the issue from other angles. The author does not intend to be dogmatic; rather, he hopes to motivate people to think through some very important topics — and thereby deepen their personal faith.

5. Finally, do all within your power (even offering rewards) to get everyone in the group to read the book. They can jot down notes for group discussion. Or, perhaps, you as the leader might provide a skeletal outline for them to fill in. Use whatever means you must to get them to read. Study groups are often stymied because of persons who neglect this out-of-class effort. Also, instruct group members not to race ahead in the book — which invariably leads to boredom, impatience, and a premature disclosure of ideas in group discussion. The rule is: *Everybody read, but everybody read together.* Your effectiveness as a teacher will, in a very real way, result from your ability to motivate adherence to this crucial guideline.

Note: Advise students to obtain these materials for sessions.

- pencil (mechanical one preferred, to eliminate the need for sharpening)
- Bible *(New International Version* or King James Version preferred, but other versions are also helpful)
- notebook (divided into two sections: "inside of class" and "outside of class")

SESSION ONE

Reading assignment: 28 pages

♦ Foreword (by Anthony Campolo, Jr.) and Preface

♦ Part One — Excellence: Need Of The World

Chapter 1 "Enough Is Enough!"
Chapter 2 "Competing Ideals: Excellence and Success"
Chapter 3 "The Greeks Had a Word for It"

Overview: The foreword and preface explain the reasons for and background of the book. The central theme is spelled out. Then, Part One focuses on the numerous ways *excellence* has been perceived in the world — and why it is so valued. Here, excellence is seen as a self-imposed standard of conduct that brings meaning, order, and fulfillment to individuals and entire societies. The key point: To understand Christian excellence, it is first necessary to comprehend how our world uses (and has used) the term *excellence*.

Foreword

Nonexcellence (and its "brothers" apathy, incompetency, listlessness, and mediocrity) exists in all areas of life. We all confront it on a daily basis.

On the chalkboard (or poster board) in your classroom, list examples of incompetency observed by your students within the last month. Expect some to be humorous and others to be upsetting.

Next, beside this list, write the *effects* or *results* — by asking each contributor to share. Example: Mechanic failed to fix car properly. Results: Car broke down, so that person was late for work (employment inconvenienced), person carried bad mood home that evening (family affected), and so on. As people share, it will be apparent that there is a ripple effect when people do things halfway.

Preface

The author admits the difficulty he had with the term *excellence* (p. 15). Then he began to define it in a more positive, helpful way. Ask class members to take a piece of paper and write down the very best definition they can think of for *excellence* (as it exists in the world). Have a time for sharing. Then try to come to a point of consensus on the very best definition that the entire class can formulate.

Chapter 1 "Enough Is Enough!"

- Invite someone into the class who is considered by the class to be truly excellent in some area. For 10 minutes allow the class to ask this person questions. Examples:

  > "What causes you to take such pride in your work?"
  > "How do you handle it when things don't go well?"
  > "How does being excellent in one area affect other areas of your life?"
  > "Can you provide some tips (attitudes as well as actions) for your excellence?"
  > "How does your excellence impact your relationship with God? Others?"

- On page 26, three truths concerning excellence are stated. Divide the class into three groups, so that each can focus on one of these truths. This is a brainstorming session in which candid reactions are welcomed. The truths can be enlarged, reduced, altered, refuted. But good reasons and examples must be given in each case. At the conclusion of the group sessions, the entire class should reassemble to hear reports (from an assigned person from each group) and to share.

Chapter 2 "Competing Ideals: Excellence and Success"

- Our nation seems very enthused about the concept of excellence, and it is mainly because of one book: *In Search of Excellence*, by Thomas J. Peters and Robert H. Waterman, Jr. Have someone give a brief review of the book. It is a good idea for this person to produce a summary sheet that encapsulates the book's content—and photocopy it for all persons in the class. Follow this up with a good discussion.

For purposes of our discussion, it should be underscored that the authors do *not* show how success and excellence are different.

- Success mania has a profound impact on the people of our country. In fact, we are all affected. As the class shares examples of this attitude, write them on the chalkboard (or poster board). Then make another list of the effects of success mania: on the nation; on ourselves as individuals.

- Have a good reader read each of the success vs. excellence differences on pages 33-34. After each, ask for a brief comment focusing on "what the author must have meant by saying that." Perhaps the class has other differences to add.

- Have class members pair off and share responses to these questions:
  "When is success damaging or destructive?"
  "When is success beneficial?"

There should be a time for sharing their ideas with the entire class.

Chapter 3 "The Greeks Had a Word for It"

- Have a class member do some pre-class research on: (a) the Greek civilization; or (b) the Olympics in ancient Greek times. This person can share his findings with the class (5-10 minutes).

Then, as the teacher, explain just how crucial the concept of excellence was for this civilization. It permeated all they did and aspired to do. It was truly the cornerstone of their civilization.

Follow this up by asking the class to share examples of other peoples or groups that seem(ed) to have excellence as their standard (e.g., Swiss).

Then bring the principle home. Ask class members to imagine the result if their Sunday-school class, church, city, or nation was thoroughly committed to excellence — the way the Greeks were.

- John W. Gardner wrote a classic book on excellence entitled *Excellence: Can We Be Equal and Excellent Too?* The following passage is often quoted from this work:

> "There may be excellence or shoddiness in every line of human endeavor. We must learn to honor excellence (indeed, to demand it) in every socially acceptable human activity, however humble the activity, and to scorn shoddiness, however exalted the activity. An excellent plumber is infinitely more admirable than an incompetent philosopher. The society which scorns excellence in plumbing because plumbing is an humble activity and tolerates shoddiness in philosophy because it is an exalted activity will have neither good plumbing nor good philosophy. Neither its pipes nor its theories will hold water."

What does this say to the Christian and his sense of calling, regardless of the kind of work he does? Focus primarily on the issue of effectiveness in witness. These issues should prompt a beneficial discussion.

Assignment

Write a letter to yourself. First, describe the degree to which you act (and feel) excellent. Also, the extent to which you act (and feel) incompetent. Tell yourself just how each of these makes you (and others) fulfilled/happy or miserable. Be very specific. Then, focusing on your most glaring weaknesses, write down specific steps you propose to take to improve these areas — with the help of our Lord. Seal your letter, address it to yourself, and give it to the teacher next week. He will mail it to you in one year.

SESSION TWO

Reading assignment: 30 pages

◆   Part Two — Excellence: Norm Of God's Word

     Chapter 4 "Understanding with An Open Mind"
     Chapter 5 "Pursuing with Fervent Heart"

Overview: Part One highlighted the importance of excellence in our world, for non-Christians and (especially) for Christians. Everyone benefits from a society that adheres to this challenging standard. Here, of course, the emphasis is on the fact of performance — doing things well, efficiently, and so on.

Part Two relates excellence to God's Word, showing how the glorious Greek ideal is vaulted to an even higher plateau. Here the focus is on attitude and motivation, because of God's power within, in addition to performance. In short, performance excellence for the right reason(s). Chapter 4 centers on conceptualizing biblical principles — to grasp what the Bible declares about God's kind of excellence. Then, chapter 5 concerns motivating ourselves to do what we need to do — in love.

Although Part One revealed some pointed differences between excellence and success, Part Two reveals even greater differences between the two.

Chapter 4 "Understanding with An Open Mind"

- What is Christian excellence in its highest and most complete sense? Page 51 makes the author's case that it is *agape* love. As the teacher, "walk" the students through the scriptural supports that the author uses to arrive at this conclusion.

   (Write these references on the chalkboard [or poster board] and encourage students to look them up in various versions.)

1 Cor. 12:31 — Introducing "Love Chapter."

1 Cor.13:13 — Love, the highest virtue (see reasons on page 51).

Ps. 8:1, KJV — Excellence describes God's very nature.

1 John 4:7 — Since God is excellence, it follows that he is love.

2 Pet.1:3 — He is the Source/Supplier of our excellence.

Phil. 4:8 — First result of his excellence within us: pure and loving thoughts (also, see Heb. 4:12 and Matt. 15:19).

2 Pet. 1:5 — Second result: loving deeds (also, see 1:10b-11; James 2:14, 17, 18b; 4:17).

Note: Explain difference between the two kinds of deeds: preparation and those that lovingly serve (p. 57).

- Divide the class into three groups. Have each group discuss, and prepare to explain to the entire class, one of the "invitations to God" (for his excellence) below:

    Confession (p. 58)

    Consecration (pp. 58-61)

    Constancy (p. 61)

  After the explanations that are made, ask for one volunteer to explain what occurred when he confessed past sins. Ask another to describe what happened when he was purged of original sin and empowered for service through consecration. Finally, ask someone to tell about his continuing journey in achieving greater constancy or Christian maturity.

Chapter 5 "Pursuing with Fervent Heart"

- Ask the class to use a sheet of paper to complete the following sentences:

    The excuses I use for not being loving (excellent) in all situations are _____

The areas in my life in which I find it the most difficult to be loving are _____

_____

_____

On a 1-to-5 scale (5 being the worst), I fall into these traps in attempting to manifest Christian excellence:

_____ see obedience to God as "painful duty"

_____ lapse into an attitude of self-righteousness

_____ am excellent in order to be better than those around me

_____ achieve excellence in one area (or with one/few persons) to the neglect of other important areas or people

_____ use excellence only as a means of attaining (what I consider to be) success

- The "gospel of success" is apparent in many areas of God's kingdom. As a group, please discuss the following questions: (Write answers on chalkboard [or poster board].)

   A. In what ways does the "gospel of success" appear in today's church?

   B. Where does the success gospel attitude lead to? Positive effects? Negative effects?

   Turn the group's attention to Cynthia R. Schaible's points on pages 66-67. Discuss.

   C. Why, in today's church, are "successful" people (high in power, privilege, prestige, and wealth) often given more honor than persons who truly manifest "Christian excellence"?

   Should this be changed/reversed? In what ways do you propose that this can be done?

   D. When is success OK for the Christian?

   Answer: When it comes as a derivative of Christian excellence rather than as an end in itself. Then the successful person can handle it wisely and share its benefits—without becoming proud or selfish.

- J. B. Phillips, author of the greatly loved version of the Bible as well as many other books, earned much money and acclaim. Like so many, it worked to his detriment. Read his testimony to the class:

  > "I was tasting the sweets of success to an almost uni-maginable degree [after writing his Phillips' translation of God's Word] ... applause, honor, and appreciation met me wherever I went. I was well aware of the dangers of sudden wealth, and I took some severe measures to make sure that, although comfortable, I should never be rich. I was not nearly so aware of the dangers of success. **The subtle corrosion of character, the unconscious changing of values, and the secret monstrous growth of a vastly inflated idea of myself seeped slowly into me** (*The Price of Success*, 9)."

  Unfortunately, Dr. Phillips entered into a severe state of depression—from which he only partially recovered before his death. In this, the final book he wrote, the sad tale is told.
  Go around the class and have each student give a one-sentence reaction to this story.
  (Key point: If this can happen to a person of the stature and spiritual depth of J. B. Phillips, that means that none of us are immune from the effects of success.)
- In pursuing excellence with a fervent heart, the book offers "God's lesson plans" from his Word. Write these on the chalkboard (or poster board).

  A. We are instructed to "approve things that are excel-lent" (Phil. 1:10, KJV).
  Note: Point out that "approve" means a total investment of ourselves rather than a simple mental assent. Also note that the phrase "things that are excellent" means "things that differ" or things that are more than "merely good" or satisfactory (p. 69).

B. God would have us study the life and teachings of his incarnate Son, who personified true divine excellence.

Note: The W. Ian Thomas quote is great to anchor this point (p. 71). Also, the one made by Edward Kuhlman (p. 70).

- Dividing into twos, have the students read the statements (p. 72) concerning why Christian excellence is so desperately needed today. Then have the pairs add reasons of their own to this list. After 5-10 minutes, have each pair share their additions as you write them on the chalkboard (or poster board).

- The final pages of this chapter refer to both "renovation" (complete renewal) and "refurbishing" (improvement of what already exists).

  Have the students make two lists. On one should be the things they need in the way of renovation, then on the other, the things needed for renewal.

  Note: Remind them that we serve a patient God, who loves us even when we fail. What's more, he provides us with his own Spirit to guide us and provide strength. (see John 14:16-17 and Ps. 36:7)

Assignment

Explain to (at least) one other person (a) what you felt that you learned from this session or these chapters; and (b) how you propose to apply what you learned to your personal life. Ask them to pray for you and to encourage you in this effort.

SESSION THREE

Reading assignment: 27 pages

♦   Part Three—Excellence: Nurtured In Our Walk

Chapter 6 "The Towel and the Cross"
Chapter 7 "Lowly, but Not Losers"

Overview: Part Three focuses on the various components of growth in excellence. Recall that after confession and consecration comes constancy or maturing in the "more excellent way." Of course, this is a lifelong process—the Holy Spirit guides, empowers, and comforts as we face new situations.

There are seven components (not steps) to consider. In a real sense, the other six emerge from servanthood (chapter 6)—the foundation of Christian love/excellence. All seven are interconnected and reinforce one another. All seven are generated by God's love/excellence placed within us. It goes without saying that they all have a critical bearing on both our spiritual well-being and our witness in the world.

Chapter 6 "The Towel and the Cross"

•   Have the class review the story of the checker player and his wife (pp. 79-80). Using the chalkboard (or poster board), have students suggest the *effects* of:
    A. the father's approach to life
    B. the mother's approach to life
(Have students share other examples they have known or heard of that are like A and B above.)

•   Turn to page 81 in the book, and focus on William Barclay's four components of servanthood. Divide into four groups, having each group discuss (and report back to the class through a representative) what each means:
    A.   inalienably possessed by God
    B.   unqualifiedly at the disposal of God

    C. unquestionably obedient to God

    D. constantly in the service of God

Note: Suggest that the groups use scripture in their explanations.

- On a sheet of paper, have students respond to these items related to the barriers of servanthood. They should do these on their own.

	Greatly Affected	*Mildly Affected*	*Not Affected*
A. unwilling to play second fiddle			
B. faking servanthood			
D. servanthood back-fires			

(For an explanation of these items, please refer to pages 83-86.)

    Depending on the mood of the group, have a discussion of the individual answers.

- Have each person pair with another and discuss specific ways they can (and will) improve in these ways—related to true New Testament servanthood:

    A. accepting inconvenient interruptions as gifts from God

    B. spiritual sensitivity to (and awareness of) others

    C. looking to God alone for reward

- Have a good reader in the class read the Ruth Harms Calkin poem on page 90. Ask each class member to give a one-sentence reaction to it. Write down key words and ideas on the chalkboard or poster board.

Chapter 7 "Lowly, but Not Losers"

- Spend a while talking about the many complexities of life— that seem to make it more difficult (even the so-called timesavers). Make a list of these on the chalkboard or poster board.

- Have each student think of a "little person made big by God" in God's Word. Then have each write a one-paragraph vita (or description of his qualities) for the job as your minister. The obvious result: Many of the personality attributes (and experiences of failure) possessed by heroes of the Bible might be seen in a negative light—by the board members of today's church.

- Ask the class:
    - A. Why does God seem to choose the weak and lowly over those who connive to gain power?
    - B. Why does God honor sacrifice more than affluence?
    - C. Why does God give a special blessing to those who express thanksgiving—in contrast to those who only demand (or beg for) more?

- Review the story of the admiral (pp. 100-101). Have groups of 3-4 discuss:
    - A. What does this story mean? (principle learned)
    - B. What does this story specifically mean to me?

- Have each person fill out a grade sheet on his internal and external simplicity.

INTERNAL	Always	Sometimes	Never
A. Prayer and Bible reading daily.			
B. Fast at least one time per week (for spiritual reasons).			
C. Thank-you list to God periodically.			
D. Read Christian book.			
E. Keep spiritual diary and write in it.			

	Always	Sometimes	Never
F. Practice the presence of God.			
G. Ask trusted friend to tell you your faults — without being defensive.			
H. Truly worship while in church service.			
I. Memorize God's Word or words of hymns.			
J. Strive for spiritual lessons in life situations.			

EXTERNAL	*Always*	*Sometimes*	*Never*
A. Give to those in need anonymously.			
B. Give faith gift to God's kingdom.			
C. Suggest ways your church can be less building conscious and more people conscious.			
D. Refuse to buy gaudy luxuries to be seen.			
E. Use cars, clothing, and appliances for longer periods of time.			
F. Do bicycle riding and walk.			
G. Refrain from eating junk food.			

H. Dedicate one "big-gift" day (e.g., Christmas) to someone in need.			
I. Will estate (portion) to God's work—and inform family.			
J. Give up comforts for spans of time.			

Have the group add items to the two lists. Discuss the results.

Assignment (options)

Commit to read the poem "My Symphony" each day this week. (Some may wish to memorize its words.) Consider it to be part of the morning/evening prayer.

Do one servant deed each day. Report the results at the start of next week's class.

Attempt to live faithfully by the internal and external suggestions listed above this week. Likewise, report to the class next week.

SESSION FOUR

Reading assignment: 29 pages

♦   Part Three — Excellence: Nurtured In Our Walk

Chapter 8 "The Joy of Unmasking"
Chapter 9 "Webs of Love"

Overview: When a person is filled with love/excellence of God, he is able to do "exceeding abundantly above all that [he could ever] ask or think" (Eph. 3:20, KJV).

Two areas where this is apparent relate to removing harmful masks (allowing true identity to be revealed) and reaching out to others to form authentic relationships.

The next two chapters discuss these crucial points.

Chapter 8 "The Joy of Unmasking"

*   Have each person turn to the person next to him and join that person in writing down the different kinds of masks we wear in life. After 5-10 minutes, have a time of sharing with the group.

*   As an entire class, discuss these questions:
    A.   What kinds of mask wearing are innocent and not harmful?
    B.   What kinds of mask wearing are especially harmful?
    (Review material on pages 108-110, writing key points on the chalkboard or poster board.)

*   Have the class read from the paragraph beginning (p. 115), "Centuries have passed since his resurrection" — over to the end of this section on page 116. Then ask each to testify to the entire group concerning Christ's complete honesty and sincerity. Each is to begin his testimony with the words: "I deeply appreciate our Lord's sincerity because _____
_____"

(E.g., he set an example for me; I can trust him at all times; he shows us how completely reliable he is; etc.)

- Each person can again turn to the person next to him and complete the sentence: "I am wearing the mask of

_____

in my life right now, and I would like to get rid of it." Have each couple, after sharing, have a word of prayer together.

Chapter 9 "Webs of Love"

- Discuss as a group (placing answers on the chalkboard or poster board): What kinds of things do we say to visitors or newcomers to our church that make them feel uncomfortable?

    Then answer the question: What statements do we make to regular attenders that should be left unsaid?

- As the teacher, take the class through the steps of rejection that Paul endured (pp. 120-122). Ask the class members to declare what they would have likely done in response to such cold treatment.

- Divide into groups and make two lists:
    A. the "maintenance-type" activities that your church (or class) is involved with
    B. the "mission-type" activities that your church (or class) is involved with
    (Then have each group give reasons for the shift of balance in one direction or the other.)
    Note: Most churches tilt in the direction of the "maintenance-type "to their own ineffectiveness.

- See the "bag of marbles" vs. "bag of grapes" contrast on pages 128-129. Have each discuss which of these your church (or class) resembles and why. Follow this up with a good discussion in class.

• Have the entire class look at the chart on page 132. Each should pick out just where he is, then where he would like to be.

Assignment

Weave a "love web" with someone that you feel especially needs friendship. Spend some time, money, and energy in doing this, and be prepared to report back to the group at the next meeting.

Employ some real creativity in this effort, but in the process be careful to be real. Also, plan to pray extensively for this person prior to and during the contact. This is crucial. Finally, do not see this as a one-week exercise—attempt to really build the foundation for a friendship.

Then *all* class members should carefully read instructions for and take the "Trenton Spiritual Gifts Analysis" (Appendix A, pp. 185-203). They should bring the result of the test with them to class next week.

SESSION FIVE

Reading assignment: 29 pages

♦   Part Three — Excellence: Nurtured In Our Walk

Chapter 10 "Refusing to Cry 'Uncle'"
Chapter 11 "We Are All Gifted"

Overview: Two additional areas are inseparably connected with authentic Christian excellence. The first has to do with an uncompromising adherence to personal convictions — because of the right scriptural reasons. The second concerns prayerfully discovering and using (with the help of the Holy Spirit) our spiritual gifts.

As these relate to Christian excellence, so they relate to one another. Holding to convictions provides freedom to serve — as the tightness of a violin string provides the musician with the ability to use that string for maximum melodic potential. Likewise, using God-given gifts can only lead to greater determination to serve him more faithfully and completely without compromise.

Chapter 10 "Refusing to Cry 'Uncle'"

*   As a group, go from one class member to the next, asking the question: What is something you detested at first but found yourself gradually getting used to — and feeling comfortable with (e.g., foods, people, jobs)?

    Follow this up by asking the group: What does this tell us about the nature of the human brain?

    (Answer: There is a definite capacity for self-deception.)

    Point out kinds of self-deception that are especially damaging (and even destructive) for people, due to this capacity we have.

*   By putting a frog in water and raising the temperature of the water only a fraction of a degree, the frog will eventually

cook. More important, he will not struggle or even be aware of his fate.

Have someone (even yourself) explain this well-known high school biology experiment to the class. Then ask persons, who are paired off with a partner, to decide how this experiment relates to sin in our lives. Save time for sharing in the whole group.

- The book mentions that some convictions are unwise to hold (pp. 137-139). Ask group members for testimonies as to who has held any of these kinds of convictions in the past. Have them be very specific.
    - A. Convictions that are little more than superstitions
    - B. Convictions that attract attention for a selfish ego
    - C. Convictions generated by an unwillingness to accept change
    - D. Convictions that are exclusively negative

- Introspection. Have members of the group respond to the two above questions on paper:
    - A. These are convictions I once had and wish that I had not let slip away.
    - B. These are convictions I once had but am glad that I no longer have.
    - C. These are convictions I've never had but would really like to cultivate.

- On the chalkboard or poster board, write the steps to compromise. Discuss each one carefully. Allow for discussion. The steps are found on page 140. (Introduce your points after referring to the illustration of the animal on a log, on the same page.)

- Go around the room, and have each student complete this sentence: The one area of compromise in my life that I intend to do something about, with God's help, is

_____

After this meaningful sharing time, pray together. As the teacher, you direct this prayer by telling students what to pray for (with pauses after each direction).

(E.g., Reflect on the damage that this area of compromise is doing in your life. [Pause] Think of how much God really wants to help you to be free from it. [Pause] Now, in faith believing, accept the fact that God is removing the desire for this and is freeing you for more complete obedience and servanthood. [Pause])

- Study these verses of Scripture that deal with compromise (pp. 141-143):
      1 Sam. 15:22
      John 15:10, 19
      Rom. 12:2
      James 1:27; 4:4
      1 John 2:15
      Rev. 3:15-16

- General discussion. Do you agree (and why) with the author's statement: "We cannot please the world and God at the same time" (p. 145)? (Support your answer.)

Chapter 11 "We Are All Gifted"

- In small groups (3-4 persons), share the results of the "Trenton Spiritual Gifts Analysis." Specifically, state what the test showed regarding your strengths and your weaknesses. Ask members of the group if they agree with the test's assessment.

- Self-evaluation. On paper, have the students answer these important questions:
      A. Which of my gifts (areas of strength on the test) am I currently using?
         In what specific ways am I using them?
      B. Which of my gifts am I not using?
         What seem to be the barriers that keep me from using these gifts?

Have a class discussion of the answers. Conclude by high-lighting the points (pp. 151-155) related to "detours" and "roadblocks."

• After pairing off, discuss the difference between a "minister" and a "layman" in God's Word. Have a report to the whole group, and then have someone summarize the ideas of James L. Garlow (p. 157).

• List the points covered in "A Needed Perspective" (pp. 160-162). Ask class members to say what each point means to them (regarding gifts).
   A. Directing primary attention to God
   B. More concerned with internal fulfillment than ex-ternal applause
   C. Continual increase in generosity

• Have a person from the church (or community) visit and share for 5-10 minutes how he uses his spiritual gifts. Ideally, this should be a few-gifts person—but someone who uses what they have been bestowed to the near maximum.

Assignment

Prayerfully decide on developing and expanding one of the spiritual gifts that you have. Think of specific ways that you can begin at once to do this. Start and record your progress. Be pre-pared to report to the group next week ... and to ask class members to encourage you in your effort, through words and prayers. (As a class, encourage one another.)

In addition, affirm at least one other person through word of mouth or note regarding his spiritual gift(s). Tell him just how much you appreciate his use of his gift. Encourage that person warmly.

Have every student take the "Temperament Test" (Appendix B, pp. 205-211) and score it before next session. Also, they should have a very thorough knowledge of the basic types of personality temperament.

SESSION SIX

Reading assignment: 19 pages

♦   Part Three — Excellence: Nurtured In Our Walk

Chapter 12 "Daring to Act"
"A Parting Word"

Overview: Knowledge that isn't acted upon becomes useless (at best) and damaging (at worst). Action requires courage, faith, and many other qualities of spirit. And it certainly involves risk. The last chapter in *Christian Excellence* focuses on the components of action taking.

Then a final word is offered to encapsulate and summarize the central theme of the book. Finally, one last appeal for Christian excellence is given.

Chapter 12 "Daring to Act"

•   Share the great story of Caleb ("Give Me This Mountain," pp. 167-169). Divide into small groups to discuss what Caleb's spirit and example says to us in our Christian walk today.

Option: Have class members complete these sentences vocally in the group:

I'd like to be a Caleb for God because _____

_____

The things that keep me from becoming a Caleb are ____

•   Have class members pair off and share what kind of temperament the "Temperament Test" revealed them to have. (It is usually a combination of the various types.) **Note:** To prepare for this sharing, write each type on the board and explain it briefly.

- Ask the class to share how each type is ideally suited to specific kinds of service for God. (Idea: Diversity of temperament is beneficial for God's kingdom. He needs us all!) Have the class be specific, and write their responses on the chalkboard or poster board.

- Discuss the points under the section, "Why Deeds Are Short-Circuited" (pp. 169-171). Which of these do the class members most identify with? Have them ranked in order of priority.
  - A. Rather talk than act
  - B. Nonassertive temperament
  - C. Unwilling to involve self in risk
  - D. Feel others will (or should) do it instead of us

- Explain the biblical metaphors related to "fighting" and "battle" (pp. 174-175). Ask the class these questions:

  - A. Why do we hear so little about agonizing and so much about comforting ourselves in the church?
  - B. In what sense can agonizing for God bring us comfort and fulfillment as Christians?

- Focus on "A Ration Pack for Doers" (pp. 176-178). Take turns and have individuals read one and say what it means to him, then another, and so on.

- The footnote (p. 178) gives "Leadership Paradoxes" that relate to the kinds of opposition we are likely to have when attempting to guide/lead people toward the right or good.

  Read them and ask the group which they most agree with. Also provide them with opportunity to cite examples.

  Knowing these facts, what can we do?

"A Parting Word"

- Review the key questions of this book with the group.
  - A. What is secular excellence (i.e., excellence from the world's perspective)?
  - B. How does secular excellence differ from success?
  - C. What is Christian excellence, and how is it spoken of in God's Word?
  - D. How does it differ from the "success gospel" that has arisen in the church?
  - E. What are the seven components of Christian excellence?

- In a general discussion, have class members tell what they received (of personal, spiritual benefit) from this book and course. Write them on the chalkboard or poster board.

- Have sentence prayers of thanksgiving, and conclude with everyone praying the ancient Hebrew prayer in unison.

  > From the conscience that shrinks from new truth.
  > From the laziness that is content with half-truths.
  > From the arrogance that thinks it knows all truth.
  > Oh, God of truth, deliver us.

  > — AMEN.